Lost (and Found) Pharaohs

Benjamin Collado Hinarejos

Cover: Gold masks of Tutankhamun and Psusennes I. Egyptian Museum, Cairo.

© Benjamin Collado Hinarejos, 2016. All rights reserved. The total or partial reproduction of text and images owned by the author without express authorization is prohibited. If you need any of these images, please contact the author.

ISBN-13: 978-1535308380
ISBN-10: 1535308389

To Angela. My wife and my support.

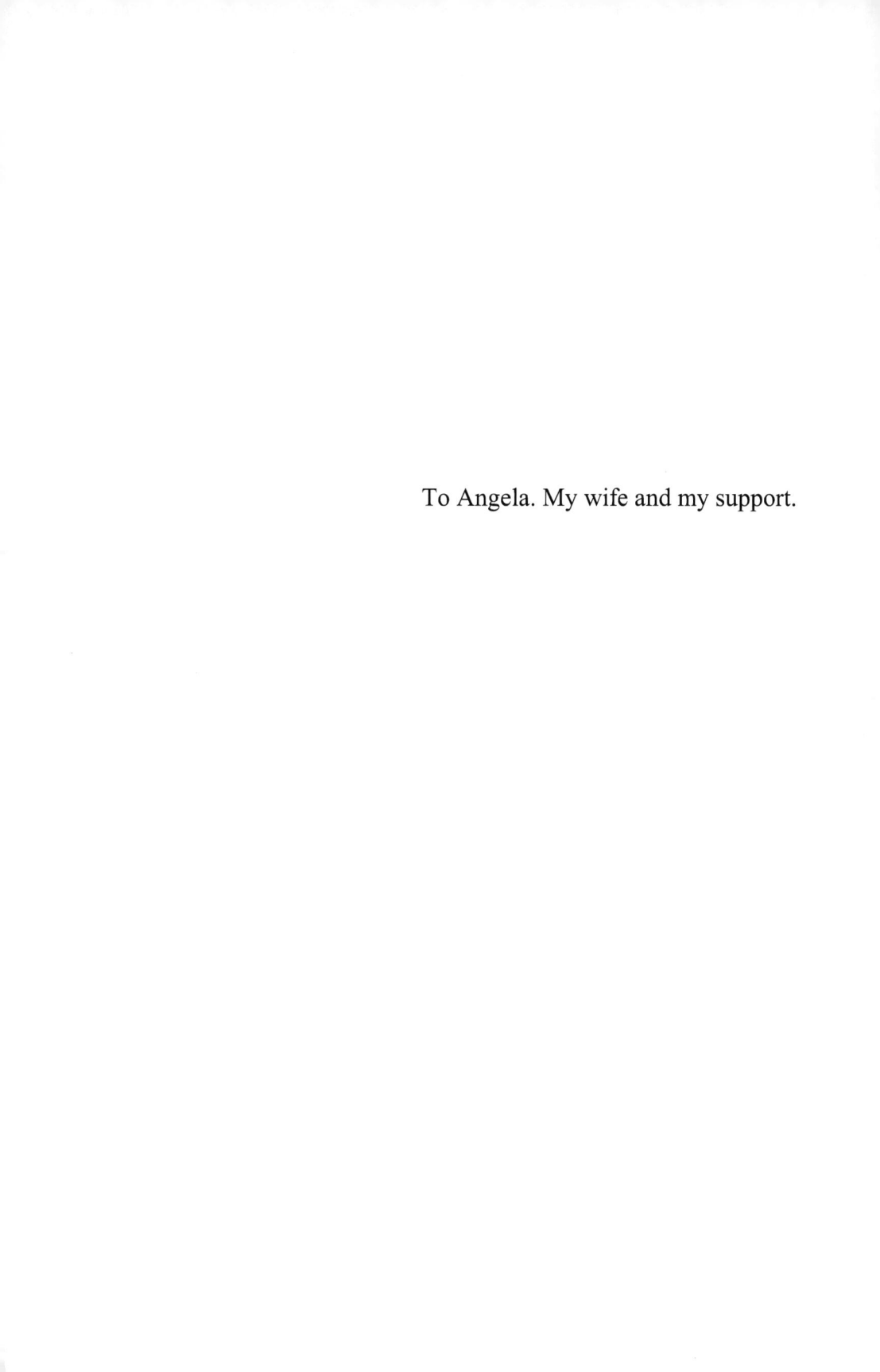

View of the Sphinx of Giza, with the Pyramids of Cheops and Chephren in the background. Photo: Félix Bonfils, late nineteenth century.

Table of content

About the Author 5

Foreword 7

FIRST BOOK 11

The Royal Mummies' Hideout 11

Introduction: The World Discovers Egypt 13

    A Frenchman to the Rescue 21

The Mystery of the Looting of the Royal Tombs 25

    The Hideout of the Monarchs 33

    What Were All Those Mummies Doing in There? 46

    For Whom Was the DB-320 Tomb Built? 53

Other Great Findings 61

    Another Royal Cachette 61

153 Mummies Seek Refuge 67

Conclusion 71

SECOND BOOK 75

Tutankhamun's Tomb and the Curse of the Mummies ... 75

First Part: Tutankhamun's Tomb 77

    Introduction. The start of an amazing adventure 77

    The First Excavations 84

But, who was Tutankhamun? 92

The Discovery of the Tomb 96

A Colossal Work 102

Growing Pains 119

The First Mummy Study, the Carnage. 127

What was the Cause of Death of the "Pharaoh Child"? 133

Is Nefertiti in KV-62? 140

Second Part: the Curse of the Mummies 145

The Beginning of Madness 145

Psychosis Spreads 150

Possible Explanations of the Deaths 156

Conclusion 161

THIRD BOOK 163

The Silver Pharaohs 163

Introduction 165

Pierre Montet and Tanis 169

Tanis 173

The Royal Necropolis and its Discovery 181

Osorkon II's Tomb 184

The Tomb of Psusennes I 188

Amenemope's Tomb..195

- The Last Secrets of Psusennes' Tomb 198
- Who were these Pharaohs? 203
  - The Third Intermediate Period and the Dynasties XXI and XXII 203
  - Tanis Burials 205
- Conclusion 211
- Bibliography: 214
  - First Book 214
  - Second Book 215
  - Third Book 215
  - Webpages: 216
- Photograps by 216

About the Author

My love for history and archeology have accompanied me since childhood, and I've been fortunate to grow up in an area rich in remains from various past cultures; something that has given me the opportunity to participate in numerous archaeological excavations in ruins of the Iberian and Roman period in Spain. I graduated in History, specializing in Ancient History and Protohistory, and so far I have published the books "The Iberians" (Akal, 2013), "The Iberians and their World" (Akal, 2014), "The Iberians and the War" (Amazon, 2014), "Tutankhamun's Tomb and the Curse of the Mummies" (Amazon, 2014), "The Silver Pharaohs" (Amazon, 2016), "Sex and Erotism in Ancient Egypt" (Amazon, 2016) and the one you have in your hands. I have also written articles for the History National Geographic Magazine and Web in Spain.

Photo from the late XIX century showing a group of Western tourists initiating the climbing to the pyramid of Cheops, helped by local guides.

Foreword

If anything could ever stir the imaginations of lovers of the ancient world, and of Pharaonic Egypt in particular, it would be the tombs and treasures left by the kings who died thousands of years ago but left their monuments behind. Such monuments have etched their names into the history of mankind, and they continue to impress us today just as much as the times in which they were built.

Of all these constructions we should highlight, undoubtedly, the great pyramids of Egypt, which are the only one of the seven wonders of the ancient world that we can still touch. Curiously, it wasn't inside of these magnificent monuments where the bodies of the pharaohs who made possible these extraordinary Egyptian constructions were found, but they were instead hidden in modest graves and dirty caves, where they managed to evade thieves throughout the centuries.

In the following pages we will review these findings that once astonished and blew the world away (although it is true that not all of them had the same media coverage). And of course, there is the most famous of all the tombs—that of Tutankhamun, the boy king— who was actually insignificant, and until 1922, an almost unknown pharaoh. Tut lived more than thirty-two centuries ago on the banks of the Nile, and became known again overnight by the hand of Howard Carter, the tenacious archaeologist whom discovered treasures worthy of a tale from the Thousand and One Nights, and who would devote almost the rest of his life to the study of the tomb and its extraordinary content.

But this discovery was not the first nor would it be the last to bring us face to face with the sovereigns whom once ruled like gods over the Egyptian people. In the late nineteenth century, at the dawn of Egyptology, and thanks to a French archaeologist—Gaston Maspero—the location was revealed of the hiding place where some of the most powerful pharaohs of all time were piled up: Ahmose I, Amenhotep I, Seti I, Ramses II, and a long list of others that left researchers speechless worldwide. Their treasures had disappeared centuries ago, but their bodies rested in peace in the bowels of the Theban mountains until they were rediscovered by a family of grave robbers, who discovered within the royal remains both a lifestyle and financial security for the rest of their lives.

The latest discovery —the Royal Necropolis of Tanis—presented the paradox of being the one that brought out not one, but three intact royal tombs, and yet was also one of the least known episodes of Egyptian archaeology. And the blame for this paradox was nothing else but war; a bloody war that not only erased the lives of men from the face of the earth, but even the memories of the pharaohs.

With this book I want to pay a modest but well-deserved tribute to all those men and women whom throughout more than two centuries of excavations and investigations have rescued from the Egyptian sands so many secrets and wonders, and to all of those who today, when archaeology in the Middle East is not going through the best of times, continue to work hard to ensure that there will still be future discoveries to come.

Important: This book includes my ebooks: "The

Royal mummies' Hideout", "Tutankamun's Tomb and the Curse of the Mummies" and "The Silver Pharaohs (The Royal Tombs of Tanis)".

FIRST BOOK

The Royal Mummies' Hideout

Lithograph by David Roberts (1796-1864) showing one of the colossi, still partially buried, located at the main entrance of the temple of Luxor in Thebes. This painter was one of the greatest popularizers of the wonders of Pharaonic Egypt.

Introduction: The World Discovers Egypt

Mummies, hidden treasures, grave robbers and curses. Few combinations may be more compelling to the general public, and if there is a place in the world where all of this truly comes together, that place is Egypt.

These elements are surprisingly intermingled in one of the most amazing and exciting archeology episodes of all time: the discovery of dozens of mummies in the cliffs of Deir el Bahari, where 3,000 years ago, pious hands hid the remains of some of the most famous pharaohs of Egypt.

Episodes like this have made the Egyptian civilization stir in the imaginations of millions of people for centuries, which has led to many people throughout history undertaking the difficult journey to the Nile country, to see with their own eyes some of the most impressive works ever created by humans. This, of course, includes the only one of the seven wonders of the ancient world that's still standing, the Great Pyramid of Giza, built as a resting place for Pharaoh Khufu.

Pharaonic Egypt ceased to exist when it was absorbed by the mighty Roman Empire which, in a gradual process known as romanization, led to the loss of their ancestral customs, religion and even their language and script, instead adopting Christianity, Latin and, only partially, the Roman way of life.

During the Middle Ages, Egypt became part of the Islamic world and closed to the West. Its ancient civilization was forgotten and almost no foreigner ventured up the Nile. The few Westerners who came to the country used to do it as a stopover on their trip to the Holy Land, so their stay was short, and they were more concerned with the few Christian vestiges than with the Pharaonic monuments, and often did not reach beyond Giza, whose pyramids were even identified with the granaries of the biblical Joseph.

The situation remained much the same until the eighteenth century, when some Europeans began to be curious about exotic objects that were offered to them by the locals and tried to see more of those impressive remains, although it was not until the nineteenth century when the real turning point was reached. At this time, Romanticism spread through Europe and North America, and the new generations looked back to the ancient ruins that connected us to the civilizations that disappeared centuries ago, not only in Europe but also, and especially, in the East. During that century the ancient Mesopotamian cultures, starting with Nineveh in 1840 were discovered, followed by Persepolis and Babylon soon later, and in the 70s, Heinrich Schliemann located Homer's Troy in the Hill of Hisarlik, in modern Turkey.

But it would seem that Egypt became the undisputed star of this resurgence of historical interest, which was possibly attributed to the 1802 book published by French artist Dominique Vivant Denon, titled The *Travels in Upper and Lower Egypt during the campaigns of General Bonaparte*, in which he describes and draws on a series of beautiful watercolors, all of which he could see when he accompanied Napoleon's expeditionary force in the adventure that led the famous French general to the land of the Nile in 1798. The book was so successful that forty editions were launched consecutively, and it was immediately translated into English and German.

Image from the book "Journey in Lower and Upper Egypt During the Campaigns of General Bonaparte" by Dominique Vivant Denon, which shows several members of the Napoleonic expedition measuring the Sphinx of Giza.

Egyptomania extended over the world, and tourists began to arrive in ever greater numbers, although only the wealthy could afford a trip of this nature, which needed not only a significant financial investment, but also a lot of time as transportation back then had to be forcibly carried aboard slow-moving sailboats first, and steam ones later, which required, for example, one week to cross the Mediterranean from Marseille to Alexandria. Not to mention intrepid travelers arriving from across the Atlantic had to be willing to endure nearly a month-long journey (if all went well) before they reached their destination.

Painting "Examination of a mummy", painted by Paul-Dominique-Philippoteaux between 1895 and 1910, in which the unwrapping of a mummy by Dr. Fouquet is shown. He is accompanied, among others, by E. Grebaut, E. Brugsch and G. Daressy. As shown, this is a scientific and social event, where several ladies are present. Private collection.

Travelers who have ventured through Egypt from antiquity to the present day can be counted in the millions, and among them were many who did not want to undertake the return journey without taking some keepsake back with them. Most settled for reproductions of smaller items like jewelry, scarabs or ushebtis (figurines that accompanied the pharaoh's tomb to replace him in the work he had to do in the afterlife); but others preferred authentic pieces and, if possible, of a larger size. Among these, one of the favorite ones in the past were undoubtedly the mummies, with or without sarcophagus. The famous British Egyptologist Amelia Edwards tells how, during one of her trips down the Nile, she was offered a mummy, which she didn't buy as she considered it to be overpriced, but other traveling companions did accept the deal, only to later throw the antiquity overboard for being unable to bear the stench it gave off. However, mummies became so fashionable among the high society of nineteenth-century London that busy evenings were organized in which the main course was the unwrapping of a mummy, to the delight of some and the horror of others.

The transportation of ancient Egyptian obelisks (giant stone pillars) highlights some of the oldest and more extreme examples of foreigners moving antiquities. This custom started already with the Romans, who shipped a large number of such pieces to Rome, where we can still find thirteen of them on display. The Italians were imitated many centuries later by the French and the British, who wanted to beautify their capitals with ancient monuments, creating astonishment among their inhabitants. We can still admire these artifacts in many European squares today, including in New York where, since 1881, the famous obelisk known as "Cleopatra's Needle" (1450 B.C.) rises for all to see.

Picture taken during a break in the visit to Egypt of the Emperor of Brazil Pedro II (seated at right, with beard) in 1871. He is accompanied by the Empress Teresa Cristina and Auguste Mariette, seated left.

But at that time the main problem for Egyptian antiquities were not tourists. Egypt was trendy, and the museums of half of the world wanted to bring its ancient treasures and exotic customs to those who could not even dream of traveling to the country of the Nile, so they would do whatever they could to get the best pieces for their collections. The consuls of countries like Russia, France, Germany, Britain, etc. were acting as true antique dealers competing for every sculpture, relief or painted wall fragment. In many cases they didn't care about the means used to get these pieces, as the end justified the means, doing shameful destruction to many monuments. As antiquity runners rushed to compete for the best prizes, they didn't hesitate to use dynamite when other less harmful means didn't yield results, or simply when they didn't want to waste time as they competed for the best pieces.

Characters like Rifaud, Belzoni and Caviglia were adventurers who traveled Egypt, sometimes on behalf of the consuls of their countries, some other times working on their own for the highest bidder, disputing the thousands of items that fueled the collections that are now exhibited in museums around the planet. And they did it with such vehemence that pitched battles between the respective teams became common as they fought over the greatest prizes. These individuals generally had no knowledge of archeology and art history, and ended up engaging in this for very different reasons. A paradigmatic example is that of Belzoni, an Italian of almost two meters tall that made a living in Europe as a fair strongman, being known as "The Titan of Padua".

Belzoni also had some knowledge of engineering, and invented a water wheel for water extraction which he presented to the viceroy of Egypt. However, his product failed to pass a testing phase, and so he had to find another occupation, whereupon he discovered the antique business, and there both his technical expertise and physical strength were truly useful, since he specialized in moving large sculptures that others had been unable to move. Like most of his colleagues he had no qualms about leaving his name chiseled into the stone of the ancient pieces he got for his clients.

Unfortunately, until well into the nineteenth century there were no serious attempts by local authorities to curb the depredations. In

1835 the Egyptian Antiquities Service was created, which would begin collecting many of the pieces that appeared throughout the country, but objects accumulated without care, first in a small building in central Cairo and later in the citadel of Saladin. When in 1855 the Archduke Maximilian of Austria visited Egypt, Viceroy Abbas Pasha had the idea to present him with all the pieces recovered so far, which meant all of the work that had been performed to accumulate these artifacts had amounted ultimately to nothing, and the work had to start again from scratch.

Portrait of Auguste Mariette, the man who tried to end the systematic looting that had plagued Egypt.

A Frenchman to the Rescue

But it would be precisely another European, Auguste Mariette, who put a stop to all these excesses, or at least tried to.

In 1850, the Frenchman had been sent to Egypt by the Louvre to locate and acquire Coptic manuscripts, but he arrived at the worst possible time. Shortly before him, two Englishmen had visited the several Coptic monasteries of Wadi Natrun, had inebriated the monks and got a good number of manuscripts without paying a single pound in exchange. The Coptic Patriarch, of course, was furious and banned the entry of any foreigners to the monasteries, and they even say he ordered to wall up the library gates completely. We don't even want to imagine the consequences for the drunken monks that allowed the looting.

Unable to get manuscripts, Mariette changed the plans on his own and, without asking for authorization from those who had sent him to Egypt, he decided to fulfill his dream and spend the money he received to conduct excavations at Memphis.

While there, and following the instructions contained in the work of the Greek geographer Strabo, he discovered in 1851 the Serapeum of Saqqara, the underground necropolis where the Apis bulls were buried. This had the effect of appeasing the wrath of the officials from the Louvre, who discovered at that moment that their money had been used on something very different from what it was intended, but nonetheless positive in its own way. The discovery also gave Mariette immediate international prestige, which he wisely used to his own benefit to get from the Turkish viceroy of Egypt, Said Pasha, his appointment as "Ma'mur", or Director of Antiquities. In obtaining this title, he had the invaluable help of Ferdinand of Lesseps, an engineer, also French, who at that time was building the country's strategic Suez Canal, and who was a close friend of the viceroy.

From the beginning of his brand new job he did anything he could to stop the looting, protect the monuments and to safeguard as many smaller pieces as could be transported. With this collection of rescued artifacts, he creates by the river port of Cairo the Museum of Bulaq, an embryo which years later would be the Egyptian Museum.

His protective mission wasn't easy, since there were many interests and big money at stake, as apart from just foreign agents, farmers had also discovered how lucrative antiquities trafficking could become, which they further considered a right that belonged to them as part of the heritage inherited from their ancestors, much more so than of the foreigners doing excavations around the country.

Of all the inhabitants of Egypt perhaps these farmers of Gurna were the busiest grave robbers of all, as nobody had it as easy as them since they literally lived on one of the necropolises of ancient Thebes. Many of them even used fresh underground tombs as pantries or rooms of their poor homes.

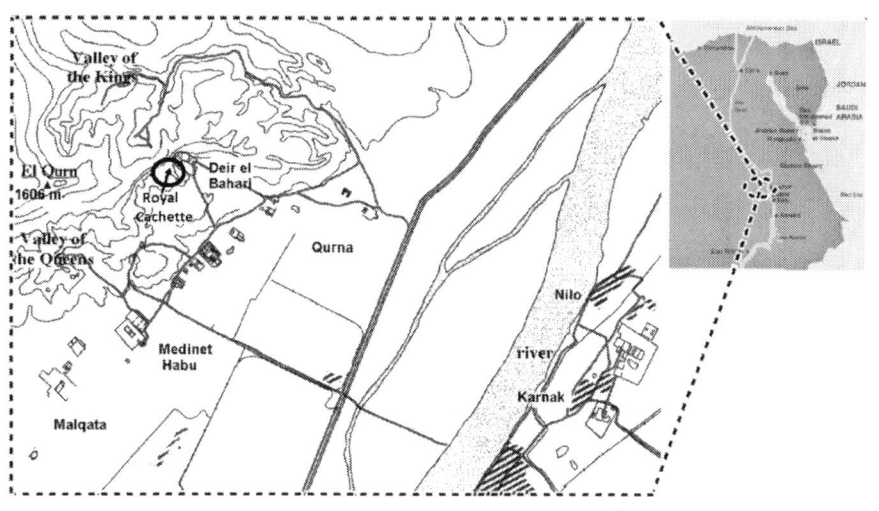

Map showing the location of the Theban necropolis area where our story unfolds.

The funerary area of Thebes, opposite to Luxor, on the west bank of the Nile, consists of three distinct areas: the Valley of the Kings, the Valley of the Queens, and the necropolis of the nobles; the latter disposed along the hillside extending between cropland and abrupt cuts delimiting the Nile valley. Qurna is built on top of these tombs, so its inhabitants didn't even have to leave home to make their clandestine excavations, a task which they accomplished quite effectively. It is impossible to know how many tombs were plundered and how many pieces disappeared after being sold to unscrupulous brokers or directly to tourists eager for a memory to take back with them and brag about in their home. And what's worse, countless objects of gold and silver, craftily decorated and elaborated with ancient designs, were gone forever after being thrown in crucibles and converted into vulgar ingots that were sold by weight.

These farmers also achieved great mastery in faking artifacts, which they sold as authentic to unwary travelers unable to distinguish crude copies. The work of counterfeiters is an activity that has continued to this day, and there are many museums, including the world's bests, which exhibit or have exhibited in their displays alleged Egyptian antiquities that in some cases are not older than their computers. I myself remember seeing on display at the National Archaeological Museum in Madrid a mummy with all the outward appearance of being real, but beside it there was an x-ray showing its interior: a simple wooden board. This alleged mummy was donated in 1887, along with other objects, from the diplomat Eduardo Toda who, of course, had acquired it under the belief that it was authentic. Years later after realizing the prevalence of so many fakes, they proceeded to take x-rays of all the mummies in the museum, discovering which were real and which were fake.

Admittedly, it was easy to "sneak" the fake one because the beautiful polychrome *cartonnages* covering the alleged mummy and showing the portrait of the deceased are indeed real, they belonged to a priest of the god Min called Nesmin, and dated to the late period. So, the value of the piece, both historically as well as by simple curiosity of such a fake, remained relevant. Although in the last remodeling of the museum, the fake mummy has been completely removed from the exhibition.

Old photograph of a couple of tourists escorted by an armed man visiting the obelisk of Sesostris I in Heliopolis, near Cairo.

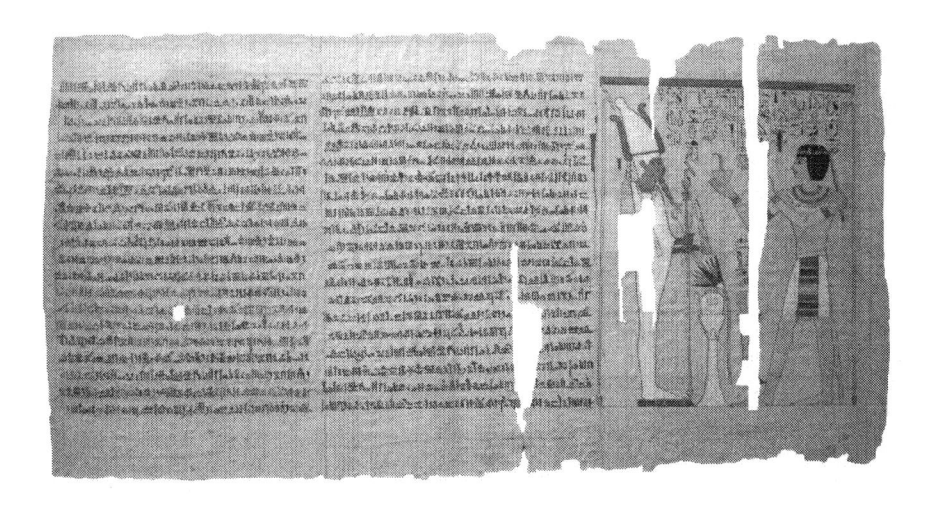

Stolen papyrus extracted from the coffin of Pinedjem II and now in the British Museum. It is one of the pieces that started the investigation of our case.

The Mystery of the Looting of the Royal Tombs

And it is at this point where our story begins, in which mingled and intertwined are tales about detectives, treasure hunting, tomb raiding, trafficking of antiquities, and mummies... many mummies. Indeed the hackneyed saying that truth is stranger than fiction may turn out to be true.

During the 1870s, a period of hard struggle for Mariette, who worked relentlessly against what was an onslaught of artifact looters and traffickers, some high-quality pieces began to appear in the active Egyptian black market and in private channels of several European countries. Whistles were blown as experts began to notice very high-quality items; highlighted among them ushabtis, decorated vessels, and, above all, some very well preserved and relevant papyri.

Already in 1870, Mariette himself had bought two papyri at Suez which had belonged to Queen Hennutaui; and which were in very good condition. However, since unfortunately the trafficking of antiquities was commonplace in those days, he did not give much importance to them.

In 1876 another papyrus, with the name of First Prophet of Amun Pinedjem II, who lived in the early tenth century B.C., and possibly the grandson of the above, was acquired in Luxor for 400 pounds by the Scottish military officer Archibald Campbell. Thinking of the papyrus as a curiosity, he sends a photo to the French Egyptologist Gaston Maspero, who had vast knowledge of Egyptian culture, and although he had never set foot in Egypt, he could read without difficulty their ancient writings. Maspero, a character who will have great importance in our history, eventually informed Mariette of the discovery, but at this point he no longer had the health and courage to initiate an investigation.

This papyrus would turn out to be very valuable. In hieratic script it displays a chapter of the Book of the Dead, and features a beautiful illustration. It can be admired today in the British Museum in London.

In 1877, a certain Saulcy refers to Maspero a photograph of another great papyrus showing the name of the queen Nodjmet, also of the XXI Dynasty. It had been bought from a Syrian interpreter who, in turn, had acquired it in Luxor. Unfortunately, and in order to obtain greater economic benefit, this papyrus was divided by its owner into three parts: one to the Louvre, one to the Egyptian Museum in Munich and another to the British Museum in London.

In the late 1880s Maspero is sent to Egypt within the French Mission, the embryo of the future French Institute of Oriental Archaeology; and in 1881, after the death of Mariette, Maspero succeeded him as director of the Department of Antiquities and of the

Museum of Bulaq, from which he decided to investigate the origin of all these items.

Photograph showing, from left to right, the Marquis of Rochemonteix, Albert Gayet, Charles Wilbour, Eduard Toda and sitting, Gaston Maspero. It was taken at the Temple of Karnak in the years 1884/1886

As he proceeded with the investigation, he concluded that one or more graves of the first magnitude, probably from members of the higher clergy, or even royalty of the XXI Dynasty, were being looted in the area of Thebes and so he ordered a thorough investigation to stop the looting before it was too late.

In March 1881 he sent a commission to Luxor that included his assistant Emil Brugsch and some friends who had accompanied Maspero to Egypt, including a former American student named Charles Edwin Wilbour. There, all the clues led to a man named Mustafa Agha Ayat as a seller of at least some of the pieces put into circulation. The problem was that he, as well as being an antique seller, also worked as consular agent for Russia, Britain and Belgium, so they couldn't act against him as he had diplomatic protection. Despite this initial setback, research did not stop and soon suspicions focused on a family of Qurna, the Abd Rassuls, since there were rumors that they might have found a royal tomb, and that they had recently built a new house; plus one of the brothers –Ahmed– also worked for Agha Ayat. Later researchers would find out that the find was an open secret known throughout the village, although it is also true that the full extent of what lay in the tomb had not even been imagined by these people, despite being used to smuggle magnificent treasures of all kinds.

In order to advance research, Wilbour posed as a wealthy American collector looking for top notch parts, and during a visit to the temple of Karnak, his guide told him about a family that could provide all kinds of objects. Of course he was referring to the Abd Rassuls. He made an appointment with Ahmed, who tried to sell him a papyrus without illustrations for 300 pounds, well above the actual value. Wilbour didn't fall into the trap, and then he showed him mummy bandages with the name of Pinedjem I. Now they were on track and the American insisted that he wanted the complete mummy. The Abdel Rassul brothers tried to trick him again with an anonymous mummy that had nothing to do with the bandages. Because of Wilbour's insistence to procure the Pinedjem mummy, Egyptians began to suspect something was amiss and refused to continue with the deal, but what were merely suspicions for Maspero and his team were now certainties, and Maspero decided to act. He reported the findings to the Egyptian authorities, and on April 4 Ahmed is arrested and interrogated by

Maspero and Brugsch. They failed to return any useful information from him, so the local authorities take over the arrest.

Mohamed Abdel Rassul at the door of his house with his family, years after starring in our history.

On the 6th of April Ahmed is sent to Qena, where he's subjected to a thorough interrogation, led personally by the dreaded *mudir* (governor) Daoud Pasha. The methods used were such that as a result, the detainee dragged a limp for the rest of his life. Yet even still he would refuse to cooperate, and so he was locked up in prison, where he spends two long months, but is finally released after not finding sufficient evidence of his involvement in the incident, as well as the many testimonies of his neighbors and some notable people endorsing the overall trustworthiness of the detainee, whom they even called *"the most loyal and selfless person of all Egypt."*

In line with this we have to bring to light the testimony which Howard Carter included in his work on the tomb of Tutankhamun, and which illustrates the real fear that the locals had of Daoud:

"One of our older workers told us about an experience he had in his youth. He had become a thief and in the exercise of his profession was arrested and brought before the mudir. It was a hot day and his nerves tensed from the start when finding the mudir relaxing in a huge clay container full of cool water. Daoud looked at him, he looked at him from that unconventional justice chair, "and when his eyes pierced me I felt my bones turn into water. Then, very gently, he said: "This is the first time you have been brought to me. You can leave, but be very, very careful not to do it a second time ", and I was so afraid that I changed my job and never saw him again."

But the arrest had brought fear and concern to the Abdel Rassul family, who were no longer calm because they knew their steps were being followed and that investigations were not going to stop there. Moreover, Ahmed wanted to be compensated for the torture received and the time he spent in prison, and so he would claim for himself half the profits from the grave, which was something that his brothers refuse, and which led to an ongoing disagreement among all of the brothers. Finally on June 5, fearing somebody else would betray them, the older brother —Mohamed— appears in Qena before the governor and confesses everything.

The *mudir* immediately warned the museum of Bulaq, but Maspero was in France, so his assistant Emil Brugsch traveled to Luxor along with the secretary of the museum, Ahmed Efendi Kamal, as well as Thadeos Matafian and Mohammed Abdessalam. Upon arrival Daoud lets them know about Mohamed's declaration and hands them several objects that the Abdel Rassuls had left on deposit, including four canopic jars of Queen Ahmose Nefertari and three papyri belonging to the queens Maatkare and Isemkheb and princess Neskons.

Mohamed Abdel Rassul at the entrance to the royal *cachette* of Deir el Bahari.

View of the current state of the entrance to the royal *cachette* of Deir el Bahari. How good the well is hidden can be appreciated.

The Hideout of the Monarchs

On July 6, 1881, Brugsch's team along with Mohamed and Ahmed Abdel Rassul headed towards the cliffs of Deir El Bahari. The road was not long but the heat of the Egyptian summer was infernal, though the expectation of a great find encouraged them. According to the brothers, they had accidentally discovered the tomb in the summer of 1871, when one of their goats got lost while grazing in the mountains. Following the sound of its bleating they located the well where the animal had fallen down, but realized they were not standing before a mere hole.

According to their statement, in order to prevent the hideout from being discovered not only by the authorities, but above all by their neighbors, they only went down to the grave on three occasions in ten years. They unwrapped some mummies to remove jewelry and amulets, and they took two or three boxes of usebthis, canopic jars, some wooden figures and half a dozen of papyrus. Objects all easy to extract, transport, conceal and sell.

But many researchers doubt the version of this casual discovery of the tomb given by the Abdel Rassul, and some believe that the discovery was made several years earlier than they recognize (perhaps in 1860). And it is very possible that they did not enter it just three times, as there are many indications that sold many other objects in addition to what they admitted, including at least one full mummy. Also, when in 2007 the Egyptian authorities finally decided to demolish the homes of Gurna to conduct excavations in the subsoil, they located about one hundred objects from this tomb hidden in various houses, which makes it clear they were not telling the truth.

But let's continue with our history. The official commission, guided by the thieves, began the climb up a winding path, as the hideout was two hundred feet above the surrounding terrain, southwest of the famous temples of Hatshepsut and Mentuhotep II. Finally they reached a small ravine at the foot of a tall crevice, and on the floor appeared an opening ten feet long and two feet wide, perfectly disguised so that it could not be seen from the bottom nor from the top of the cliff. They placed a palm trunk they had brought across it, and with a rope attached to the trunk, they brought Mohamed down the nearly thirteen foot drop, followed by Brugsch. After lighting torches, both were introduced to a narrow passage less than five feet wide and partially filled with the sand that accumulated inside of it, which required them to nearly crawl on their knees.

The first thing Brugsch saw upon entering the corridor was a coffin in white and yellow with the name of Nebseni, which was just over two feet from the entrance. Further away, more coffins were discovered, including one coffin that reminded him of the style of the seventeenth dynasty, a second that he identified as belonging to Queen Hennutaui, and a third belonging to none other than Seti I. The German believed he was dreaming.

In addition to the coffins, there were many other objects half-buried in the sand. Brugsch himself described it as follows:

"Funerary porcelain offerings, metal and alabaster containers, fabrics and trinkets, until, on reaching the bend in the corridor, I saw so many coffins that my legs were shaking, when I calmed down, I examined them as best I could to the light of my torch, and saw they contained royal mummies of both genders, and that was not all. I kept walking and came to another chamber in which, against the wall or floor, there were a number of large and heavy coffins. I saw the excitement in my face reflected in their golden polished surfaces and I had the feeling I was watching the faces of my own ancestors".

The first section of the passage is 24.27 feet long, and eventually turns at right angles to the north, and opens to a long and irregular tunnel 78 feet and 5.9 feet high and between 4.26 and 6.5 feet wide. At the end of the tunnel there is a steep slope that is saved by five or six steps crudely dug into the rock. At that point is observed on the west side a large niche about five meters long and three meters deep, in what looks like the start of a new gallery or chamber that was never continued.

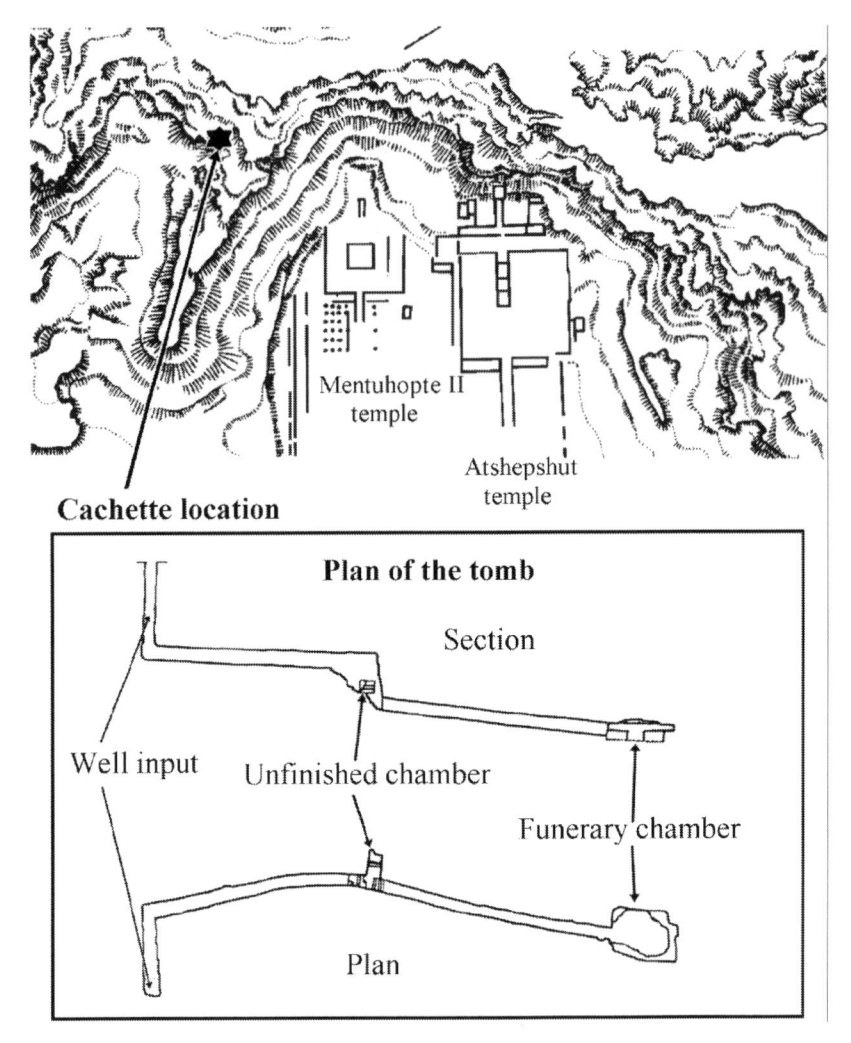

Plan of the DB-320 tomb and its location with respect to the most famous monuments of Deir el Bahari.

Once on the lower plane there continues a tunnel similar as above along another 100.3 feet, until ending in a chamber of rectangular tendency of about 26.24 feet long and a maximum height of 5.64 feet, but on the sides it's a bit lower because it has bench-like carvings, leaving in the middle an oblong irregular surface.

The whole tomb appeared to the explorers as a chipped

excavation, with unkempt aspects, like rough walls and an overall irregularly shaped layout. It was far in comparison from the condition of the royal tombs of the nearby Valley of the Kings.

The original telegram sent by the governor to Cairo said that, according to Mohamed, there were about 40 sarcophagi total and that in many of them there appeared a cobra as worn by pharaohs on the forehead. Brugsch was perplexed; in the flickering torchlight he continued reading the names of the kings who rested there: Ahmose I, Thutmose III, Ramses I, Ramses II; He was face to face with some of the greatest pharaohs of Egypt's history. And there were still many coffins left for reviewing!

His eyes darted from one corner to another, and in the two hours in which he was touring the galleries again and again, on more than one occasion having to literally climb on piles of sarcophagi, he kept noticing countless pieces that by themselves, would have justified a campaign of excavations; however there were hundreds if not thousands of such items (the final tally approached 6.000 pieces salvaged, plus 42 mummies).

But suddenly a realization fell on his mind like a sledgehammer. They were alone in the middle of the mountain, and the nearest town was a nest of thieves who for centuries lived of looting cemeteries. By now it was more than likely that word would have gotten out that they were in the tomb that was discovered by Abdel Rassul. Surely the imagination of the villagers would have overwhelmed them with thoughts of chests full of gold and precious stones and immense treasures that foreigners were preparing to snatch. The possibility that at any time a crowd of men, women and children, or even real bands of robbers would show up, all willing to take the findings by force, was not only real, but more than likely. Because for those starving peasants these were still their treasures, their heritage ... their bread.

Brugsch realized it was necessary to take everything out of there and to do so fast. There was no time for anything else, so it is that Brugsch sent one of his aides to inform Daoud Pasha of the magnitude of the find, request support and then recruit workers from the nearest populations. Soon he brought together about three hundred men willing to earn a wage, even at the cost of losing a fortune that would soon be sailing down the Nile to Cairo. Meanwhile, the governor made available a large group of men, who would be responsible mainly for surveillance of workers in order to avoid bad temptations.

But as the saying goes, rush is not a good counselor. Although Brugsch was the photographer from Bulaq's museum, he didn't take a single photograph nor even made a brief outline of the exact position of the pieces in the galleries, so a lot of information got lost forever because the positioning of objects on planes projected later was based on the memories of the few who were there, especially the Abdel Rassul brothers. This makes the accuracy conspicuous by its absence, and left many doubts about whether the sarcophagi locations were fully accounted for. To top it all, they overlooked inscriptions that had appeared on the walls of several points of the galleries with indications of transfers of some of the mummies, and made by those who carried out such transfers. Some texts were collected afterwards, but others were lost forever due to the collapses of the unstable cavern.

Once workers were ready, they selected the men who were considered more trustworthy to help them remove objects from the tomb under the close supervision of Mohammed Abdessalam. Meanwhile, Emil Brugsch and Kamal Ahmed Efendi received them at the top of the well, packed them in the best way possible and moved them to the foot of the cliff, a task that required a great deal of vigilance.

Engraving done in London in 1882 where a recreation of the transfer of the coffins from the royal *cachette* is shown. On the painting, a portrait of one of the protagonists of our history, Emil Brugsch.

This task was completed in just forty-eight hours. To get an idea of the haste with which everything was done and the unsuitable way in which they worked, we remember when in 1922 Howard Carter discovered the tomb of Tutankhamen, it took him eight weeks just on emptying the antechamber to reach the door of the funeral chamber itself, and the work of inventory, consolidation, packing and moving all the material found in the tomb took Carter and his team no less than ten years.

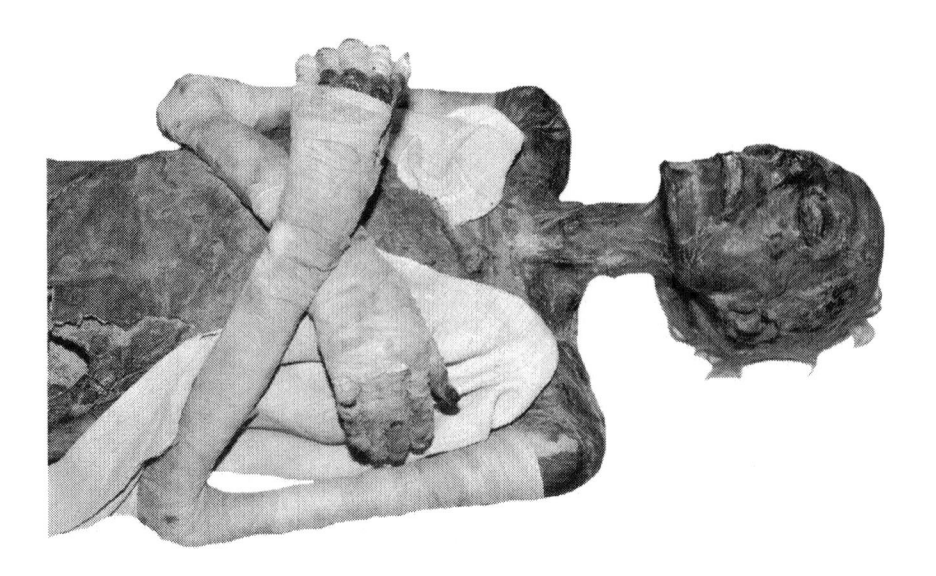

Unwrapped mummy of Pharaoh Ramses II, one of the best preserved mummies located in the royal *cachette* of Deir el Bahari.

When all objects were out of the tomb, at the foot of the cliff, a long, strange procession was launched under the hot desert sun. Long lines of men carrying boxes, bags and many sarcophagi, some so big that they needed up to sixteen men to transfer, slowly marching across the plain of Thebes and along the banks of the Nile to reach Luxor eight hours later. Throughout the transfer there were several detected attempts to smuggle parts by porters, who harbored the hope that among so many objects the theft would go unnoticed, but the foreman and his assistants kept their eyes wide open, and used sticks to flog the would-be smugglers so that they managed to recover almost everything that was attempted to be stolen. Although not everything survived the transfer, and we must mourn the passing of a basket containing fifty ushebtis made of blue faience. On the afternoon of July 11 the improvised caravan had arrived at Luxor, but still had to wait there for three days until the requested boat arrived from Cairo which could transport their precious cargo.

Maspero recounted the scene:

"As soon as we loaded it on board, it left to Boulak with its cargo of kings. Curiously, from Luxor to Kuft, on both banks of the Nile, the fellahin women followed the boat, disheveled, screaming, and the men fired their rifles as is customary to do so at funerals".

What we don't know is whether these melodramatic gesture were because the peasants tried to honor their ancient kings, or actually lamented the enormous wealth they saw disappear downstream.

Another lesser known story focuses on the intricacies of the bureaucracy. When the ship arrived to Cairo, customs employees did not know how to classify the more unusual cargo, which did not fit any of the categories set out in their forms, so the mummies were recorded in customs documentation as "Farseekht", i.e. dried fish. I doubt that this classification would have been welcomed by kings such as Sheti I or Ramses II, who used to be no less than the masters of the world, true gods on earth.

Once the shipment landed in Cairo, it was transferred to the museum of Bulaq, where new rooms had to be built hastily in which to accommodate the new tenants, and where a long process of study and identification began. One of the main problems encountered by researchers was that in the course of successive transfers and restorations performed on the royal mummies in ancient times, they had been changed of coffin more than once and some ended up in reused sarcophagi very different from their own that often had been destroyed. As a result, the mummies sometimes did not match the names on the outside of the coffins.

Gigantic wooden coffins from the *cachette* of Deir el Bahari. To the right, the one belonging to Ahmose-Nefertari, and to the left that of Ahotep. Still in the old museum of Bulaq.

Some mummies even had to be bandaged again by priests after being unwound by grave robbers who sought valuable jewelry and amulets that were hidden among their bandages, which was a very typical custom of the ancient Egyptians that considered these amulets as essential to protect the deceased. As in so many other aspects of the funeral world, this custom was taken to the limit by the Pharaohs, who covered themselves with a complete magical armor (on Tutankhamun's mummy a total of 143 objects were found). And so the Pharaohs themselves were partly responsible for the damage of their bodies by attracting the greed of the looters seeking the treasures they hid literally glued to their bodies. All this commotion caused, on more than one occasion, a confusion about the identities of the bodies when the priests had to re-bandage them.

Detail of the coffin containing the remains of Seti I, where the text written by the priests can be seen in which the occupant is identified and the vicissitudes of his transfer narrated.

The result is that, quite often, the true identity of the bodies would be unknown and doubt was cast upon all of the subjects about whether the names, bandages and mummies corresponded to reality, as significant differences were often detected. For example, the age of death of some of these pharaohs, when tested with current technologies and compared to the years of reign assigned to them in monuments and ancient lists came up incongruent. For example, the study of the mummy of Tuthmosis III indicates that he died at 35-40 years of age, while sources indicate that he reigned at least 55. The data does not match, and worst of all, it's not an isolated case.

In recent years DNA tests have begun to be conducted on the preserved mummies, which apart from helping to elucidate the true family relationships between pharaohs, queens and descendants assumptions, surely will yield a few surprises on the identities of more than one of the best known mummies.

Sometimes the ancient priests themselves who were responsible for making transfers and restorations of mums are the ones who help archaeologists in the present, providing crucial information for identification purposes. It is quite common to find, written in his own hand on the outside of some of the coffins, the narration and records of the body that the coffin contains; such as the date in which the operations were carried out and by whom. As already stated, on the walls inside this tomb some graffiti were found made by those who carried out the transfers which described a detailed log of all the different operations performed by the priests. Unfortunately, most of these very important texts have been lost by landslides. A few years after the discovery of the tomb, there was an attempt to access it again to document it, but the cave proved too dangerous to try. After several failed attempts, in 1998 a Russian-German team finally achieved access to the old tomb. Surprisingly, over 100 years after its discovery, parts of objects and inscriptions in the walls were still recovered, forgotten by the nineteenth-century diggers.

In late July 1881, the discovery of the cache of royal mummies of Deir el Bahari (dubbed tomb DB-320) was released to the world in Paris, and on September 15 in Berlin, under the International Orientalists Congress, causing a stir among Egyptologists around the world, who not even in their dreams imagined to meet face to face with some of the most famous kings of Egypt who ruled the land of the Nile during one of its periods of greatest splendor.

In an attempt to encourage other grave robbers to share their secrets, Maspero rewarded Mohamed Abdel Rassul 500 pounds and also hired him as foreman of the excavations to be developed in Thebes, since he was convinced that if he put so much effort in his new job as in his previous activities, it would give him much joy, something that would be confirmed a few years later, as we shall see at the end of this work.

Four usebthis from the hideout of Deir el Bahari on display at the National Archaeological Museum in Madrid.

What Were All Those Mummies Doing in There?

One of the first questions that come to mind when knowing this story is why were all these mummies gathered there, and not in their graves? The answer cannot be simpler, because the latter had stopped being safe a long time ago.

And we are not talking about the danger of looting by Westerners, who at the time of discovery had already spent many decades digging every corner of Egypt, but another much older, dating back to almost the same moment in which the burials took place.

Because the history of the royal tombs in ancient Egypt runs parallel to their plunderers, this is why it's so difficult to find an intact tomb. Throughout the centuries, the royal architects introduced numerous improvements in their quest to avoid desecration: deep wells, giant stone gates to seal the passageways, labyrinths, traps, etc, but it was all in vain.

Changes in the typology of the tombs would not be, in some cases, more than just an attempt to combat this danger. That, for example, is believed to be one of the main reasons why during the New Kingdom pharaohs not only stopped burying themselves under the pyramids, but separated the royal tombs from their temples. Until then, funerary temples had been next to the pyramids, and thus very close to the deceased, as the ancient Egyptians developed there a series of rites and ceremonies that they considered necessary for their resurrection in another world.

But from the beginning of the XVIII Dynasty (about 1550 B.C.), although mortuary temples continued to be constructed at the edge of the Nile valley as before, the royal tombs moved more than mile a away, to the area known to us as the Valley of the Kings (the ancient Egyptians knew it as *Ta-Sejet-Âat*, the Great Meadow), an inhospitable dryland formed by two former water courses surrounded by high mountains, with difficult access through a narrow but easy to navigate path. We do not know for sure why the site was chosen, although it may have to do with the fact that this place is dominated by a mountain –the El Qurn– whose shape is reminiscent of a pyramid. In a way, perhaps the Pharaohs believed they were still being buried under a pyramid.

The first tomb we know in the Valley is that of Thutmose I, and we have many details on its construction, since its architect –Ineni– left in his own tomb a narration of the work, emphasizing that he succeeded in keeping the status of the tomb in absolute secrecy. But it is very likely that his predecessor, Amenhotep I, became buried there in the tomb called KV-39 (King Valley-39). From him, most of the pharaohs of dynasties XVIII, XIX and XX had their tombs dug in here.

Those responsible for its construction were a small group of skilled workers, for which their own village was raised very near from there —The Place of Truth— which is known today by its Arabic name Deir el-Medina. In the village lived all the trades needed for the construction of the royal tombs: excavators, painters, sculptors, woodcarvers, goldsmiths, etc. These artisans lived in much more favorable conditions than those of other Egyptians at the time. Yet, interestingly it was here that were seen the first strikes of which we are aware in history, when these workers refused to go to work if they did not get their wages paid, consisting mainly of food.

But despite all these precautions theft didn't cease with the new location of the tomb. This can be seen perfectly in the famous tomb of the boy king Tutankhamun, of the Eighteenth Dynasty, which suffered two intrusions it seems only ten or fifteen years after his burial, but these intrusions were discovered and the tomb resealed again.

Although, as we see, thefts had begun much earlier, the bulk of the spoils would occur from the XX dynasty, especially during the so-called Third Intermediate Period (approx. 1070-655 B.C.), a period of decline and crises both economically and politically, when the power of the pharaohs decreased and were unable to control such vast empire. In fact, they only effectively ruled the north, the delta area, from the capital of that era established in Tanis, while in the south the real rulers were the priests of Amun, from their center of power in the temple of Karnak. During this period the builders of royal tombs were left jobless, and the town of Deir el-Medina was abandoned.

And these thefts would not be carried out only by simple tomb robbers, but also by the guardians themselves and workers of the necropolis, senior local officials, priests and even by the same pharaohs, who appropriated large amount of valuables stolen from the graves of their ancestors. This can be checked in the tombs of dynasties XXI and XXII such as Pharaoh Psusennes I, who reigned between about 1040 and 992 B.C., and who was located at Tanis buried in a sarcophagus of red granite that had belonged to Merneptha, a king of the Nineteenth Dynasty. Or the First Prophet of Amun Pinedjem I, whose mummy appeared in the hiding place of Deir el Bahari in a coffin built for Tuthmosis I, although this last pharaoh was also located buried in the same grave.

We are fortunate to have several ancient papyrus in which charges for robberies in tombs are registered, and even the trials that followed. The most famous case, from the time of Ramses IX, is described by Howard Carter in his book about the tomb of Tutankhamun, and very briefly summarized here: The story involves Khamwese, vizier of the district of Thebes, Peser, mayor of East Thebes, and Pewero, mayor of Western Thebes—who was responsible for monitoring the necropolis. Peser receives information of widespread thefts in the Theban necropolis and immediately informs the vizier. With this he expects to undermine the prestige of the mayor of the west bank, with whom he has very bad relations. But he makes a mistake listing the exact number of desecrated graves; ten royal tombs, four tombs of priestesses of Amun and a long list of tombs belonging to individuals.

The next day the vizier sends a commission to investigate the necropolis and this confirms that all listed individual tombs have been violated, though only two of those belonging to priestesses and only one of the royal tombs. Surprisingly, in the trial it was considered that the claim was false since the figures did not match, with which Pewero becomes free of guilt and decides to take revenge on his accuser. He organizes a demonstration with all workers in the necropolis, and this passes, casually, in front of Peser's house. Peser again commits a reckless act by facing the protesters, threatening an officer before numerous witnesses to report them directly to the pharaoh. Now Pewero seizes the opportunity and denounces Peser to the vizier for wanting to skip his authority by attempting to go directly to the king, which is considered a contempt for the vizier.

Result: Peser went from complainant to accused in a trial in which he himself, by reason of his position, had to participate as a judge and plead guilty to perjury.

When analyzing in depth the trial details collected in the papyri, it is more than clear that both Pewero as well as the vizier Khamwese were beneficiaries of the spoils from looting, if not their direct promoters.

Other papyri give us another trial account a few years later, in which eight men are accused of looting a royal tomb. We even know the names and occupations of five of them: the woodcarver Hapi, Iramen the artisan, Amenenheb the peasant, Kemwese the waterboy and Ehenefer the slave. According to these texts the interrogation began as usual in those days, "with a double reed, slamming their hands and feet." This immediately refreshed the memory of one of the detainees, who confessed the following:

> "We opened their coffins and the wrappings they were in. We found the August mummy of this king ... There were many amulets and ornaments of gold around his neck; his face was covered with a

golden mask; the August mummy of this king was completely covered in gold. The wraps were wrought with gold and silver on the outside and inside, encrusted with all manner of precious stones. We took all the gold that was in the August mummy of this god, and amulets and ornaments around his neck as well as the shroud in which he rested. The Queen appeared on a similar provision and we stripped her the same way. We burned the shrouds. We stole the objects we found, vessels of gold, silver and bronze. We divided the gold found on these two gods, on their mummies, the amulets, ornaments and wraps, into eight parts"

Another striking example is found in the Leopold-Amherst papyrus preserved in two parts in museums in Brussels and New York, where the confession of the stonemason Amenpanufer is recounted during the process:

"We headed to rob the tombs as our regular habit, and found the tomb of the pyramid of King Sejemreshedtawy, son of Ra, Sobekemsaf II, which was not at all like the pyramids and tombs of the nobles whom we regularly steal from. We took our copper tools and made our way up the pyramid of the king through its interior. We found their underground chambers, grabbed lit candles and moved forward. Then we went through the rubble and found the god lying in the back of his burial site. And we find the burial place of Queen Nubjaas, his queen, located next to him. We opened the coffins and caskets in which they were in, and found the royal mummy of the King equipped with a sword. We gathered the gold found in the noble mummy of the King, along with amulets and jewels that were in his neck. Similarly we gathered all we found on the mummy of the Queen, and set fire to their coffins. We took the furniture we found with them".

No better descriptions could be found of such robberies and the vain attempts to tackle them, although the punishment waiting these defilers of the royal tombs could not be more frightening: impalement.

In those moments of widespread insecurity, it would be the priests of Thebes who, in an attempt to secure eternal life for the Pharaohs, decided to transfer the mummies and the remains of their grave goods that had not been looted to secure locations without leaving the Valley of the Kings, thus making it easier to concentrate their surveillance forces. These hiding places are known as *Cachettes*.

For example, it is known that the remains of Ramses III's were moved at least three times, and in the sarcophagus of Ramses II the following inscription appears:

"Year 17, third year of the second season, day 6 of the transfer of Osiris, King Usermare-Setepnere (Ramses II), to his new burial in the tomb of Osiris, the King Menmareseti (Seti I), by the high priest of Amun, Pinedjem".

A few years later both Seti I and Ramses II were brought to the tomb of Queen Inhapi, where they remained until their final transfer by Pinedjem to the *cachette* of Deir el Bahari.

Presumably the other mummies found in the royal *cachette* would suffer a similar pilgrimage.

Lids of the inner and outer coffins of the First Prophet of Amun Pinedjem II. Quite possibly he originally built this tomb for his wife, but finally it became a makeshift royal refuge. Egyptian Museum in Cairo..

For Whom Was the DB-320 Tomb Built?

The issue of who this tomb was built for is still not definitively closed, but recent research indicates that it was built by Pinedjem II for his wife Neskons, though after her, it was also used to bury Pinedjem himself and the rest of his family. Unlike the rest of the sarcophagi, the ones of this family are practically intact and an important part of their grave goods have been preserved, in spite of many of the objects that were initially sold in the antiquities black market and whose sale led to the initiation of investigation to locate this *cachette*, originated from this group of mummies. We don't know how many artifacts from this tomb were sold by the Abdel Rassul family and disappeared without a trace.

Another hypothesis considers that the tomb was originally built for Queen Ahmose Inhapi of the seventeenth dynasty, as is indicated by the presence of both her body and her original sarcophagus, something unusual in the rest. But the truth is that it doesn't seem very logical that if this queen was the first occupant of the tomb, her body would appear near the entrance and not in the burial chamber, which as mentioned above, was occupied by Pinedjem and his family.

A third possibility is that it was originally a little grave for Amosis Inhapi, which was extended by Pinedjem II to serve him as family burial, and which was accompanied by a vast legion of displaced pharaohs.

Mummies Located in the Royal Hideaway

- **Sekhenenre Tao II,** Pharaoh of the XVII Dynasty
- **Ahotep,** of the XVII dynasty, wife of Sekhenenre Tao II.
- **Ahmose-Inhapi,** of the XVII Dynasty, wife and sister of Sekhenenre Tao II.
- **Ahmose-Hentimehu,** of the seventeenth dynasty, daughter of Sekhenenre Tao II and Ahmose-Inhapi.
- **Ahmose-Sitkamosis,** princess of the XVII Dynasty, probably daughter of Pharaoh Kamose. Her mummy was inside a coffin with the name Pediamun.
- **Ahmose I,** Pharaoh founder of the XVIII Dynasty, son and brother of Kamose Sekhenenre.
- **Ahmose-Nefertari,** from the XVIII Dynasty, daughter of Sekhenenre Tao II and Ahotep, and wife of Ahmose I. Within this

gigantic sarcophagus, of over three meters long, there was another mummy belonging to an unidentified woman, whose rapid degeneration forced it to be buried after a cursory examination.

- **Ahmose-Meritamun,** of the XVIII Dynasty, daughter of Ahmose I and Ahmose-Nefertari.

- **Siamon,** of the XVIII Dynasty, son of Ahmose I and Ahmose-Nefertari.

- **Sitamon,** XVIII Dynasty, daughter of Ahmose I and Ahmose-Nefertari. This mummy was destroyed in antiquity, preserving only the skull. The priests then made a false body with sticks and fabric which they then wrapped in dressings giving it the appearance of a real mummy.

- **Ahmose-Sapair,** prince of the eighteenth dynasty, son of Ahmose I and possibly Ahmose-Nefertari.

- **Amenhotep I,** Pharaoh of the eighteenth dynasty, son of Ahmose I.

- **Tuthmosis I,** Pharaoh of the eighteenth dynasty. There are many doubts about the true identity of this mummy.

- **Thutmose II,** Pharaoh of the eighteenth dynasty.

- **Thutmose III,** Pharaoh of the eighteenth dynasty. His mummy had been desecrated in antiquity and broken into three pieces, so that when they restored it, priests tied four small wooden oars around it to give it strength.

- **Baket,** probably Baketamon, of the XVIII Dynasty, daughter of Thutmose III.

- **Rai,** of the XVIII Dynasty, nurse of Ahmose-Nefertari.

- **Sheti I,** Pharaoh of the XIX Dynasty.

- **Ramses II,** Pharaoh of the XIX Dynasty.

- **Ramses III,** Pharaoh of the XX Dynasty.

- **Ramses IX,** Pharaoh of the XX Dynasty.

- **Nebseni,** of the XX Dynasty, scribe and father of Tentamón possibly wife of Ramses XI.

- **Pinedjem I,** of the XXI Dynasty, First Prophet of Amun. His mummy was in the tomb of Thutmose I.

- **Hennutaui,** of the XXI Dynasty, wife of Pindejem I.

- **Masaharta,** of the XXI Dynasty, First Prophet of Amun, son of Pinedjem I.

- **Tayuheret,** of the XXI Dynasty, singer of Amon and possibly wife of Masaharta.

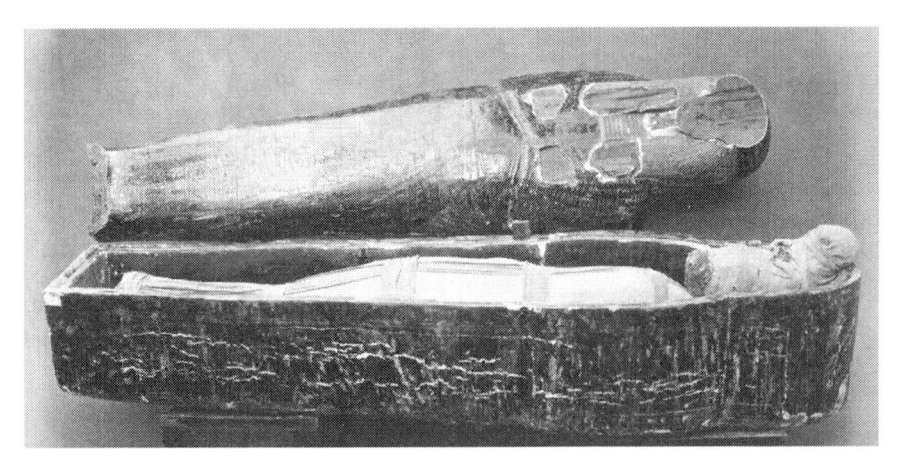

Coffin containing the mummies of Maatkare and newborn daughter, Moutemhat. Quite possibly both died during childbirth.

- **Maatkare,** of the XXI Dynasty, daughter of Pinedjem I. She must have died in childbirth along with her newborn daughter, Moutemhat, accompanying her, also mummified in the same coffin.

- **Pinedjem II,** of the XXI Dynasty, First Prophet of Amun.

- **Isemkheb,** of the XXI Dynasty, daughter of Menkheperre and wife of **Pinedjem II.** Her mummy is well preserved and is the only one in the tomb that has not been unwrapped.

- **Neskons,** of the XXI Dynasty, niece and wife of Pinedjem II.

- **Nesitanebetashru,** of the XXI Dynasty, daughter of Pinedjem II.

- **Djed Pthahiufankh,** of the XXI Dynasty, Third or Fourth Prophet of Amun, married a daughter of Pinedjem II.

- **Nodjmet,** of the XXI Dynasty, wife of Herihor.

- **Unknown Male E.** It is believed that he could correspond to Pentaure, of the XX Dynasty, son of Ramses III.

- A coffin on the name of Mashonttimthou containing actually a fake mummy made of fabric bundles that shaped the body.

- There are **another seven anonymous mummies** of which no data can be provided.

- A wooden box with the name of Queen Hatshepsut contained a tooth and an organ (possibly a liver) mummified. This tooth has proven of enormous importance, since in June 2007, then Secretary General of the Supreme Council of Antiquities, Zahi Hawass, announced with great fanfare that through it, it had been possible to identify this famous queen. The search became a modern and somewhat macabre version of the tale of Cinderella, but using dental analysis.

They had a tooth, apparently of Hatshepsut, and several possible unidentified royal mummies, so a study of these bodies was performed using tomography (CT) to find a mummy with a hole in its jawbone where the tooth would fit. Finally they discovered that one of the two female mummies found in 1903 by Howard Carter in the tomb known as KV-60, in the Valley of the Kings, was missing a tooth, but retained some of its roots. The tooth found in the cachette of Deir el-Bahari fit exactly within the jaw and roots of the mummy in the Valley of the Kings, so the identification of Hatshepsut was completed.

Seated statue of Queen Hatshepsut on display at the Metropolitan Museum of Art in New York.

Sculpture of Amenhotep II making an offering. Tomb KV 35 was built for this king. Egyptian Museum of Turin.

Other Great Findings

Another Royal Cachette

The DB 320 was the first royal *cachette* located but not the only one. Just a few years later, in 1898, the French archaeologist Victor Loret would discover that inside the tomb of Amenhotep II (KV 35) there were many more pharaohs also buried.

Sarcophagus of Pharaoh Amenhotep II, still containing the mummy inside. As seen, it had been unwrapped by thieves.

As soon as Loret entered the tomb, he had the wits scared out of him as he was confronted, right at the entrance, by a mummy stripped of its bandages, lying on a ritual boat, seemingly staring at him from through the flickering candlelight. The researchers believed that this could be the body of Pharaoh Setnakht, whose coffin was one of the group of nine that they later found in a side room of the tomb, but was now occupied by another mummy. Thieves had stripped amulets and jewelry hidden between his bandages and thrown him onto the wooden boat, where Loret found him.

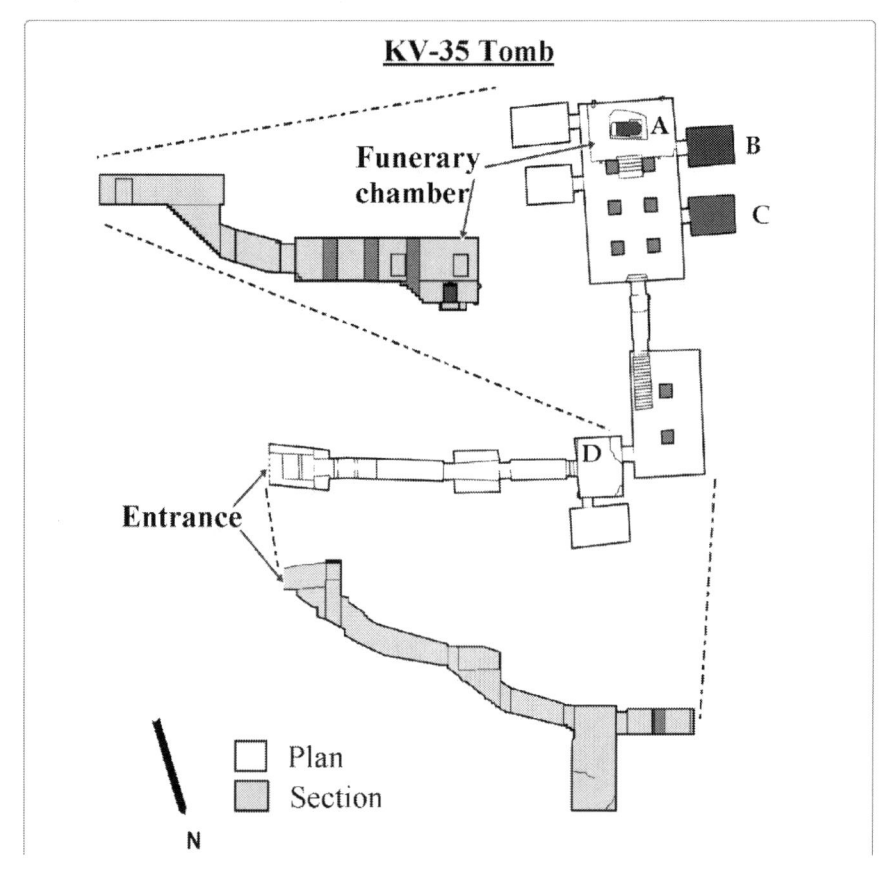

Plan and section of the tomb of Amenhotep II (KV-35). A, burial chamber. B, room where the three unwrapped mummies were found. C, room where the nine mummies were found. D, place where the mummy on the ritual boat was found.

As was previously mentioned, at the bottom of the tomb in a side walled room, archaeologists found nine coffins, all painted gray and some reused, in which rested eight kings of the XVIII, XIX and XX dynasties: Ramses IV, V and VI, Tuthmosis IV, Seti II, Amenhotep III, Meremptah, Siptah and an unknown woman who could be the queen Tausert. Furthermore, in another room Loret found three other mummies without their bands: an elderly woman who most researchers consider is the queen Tiy, a boy of about eleven years with the pigtail of princes perfectly preserved, who could be either the Prince Thutmose, son of Amenhotep III and Tiye, or prince Webensenu son of Amenhotep II; and a third mummy belonging to a relatively young woman who has created much controversy, having been identified by the once all-powerful Zahi Hawass as the mother of Tutankhamun, while recently a British researcher has hypothesized that she is actually Queen Nefertiti.

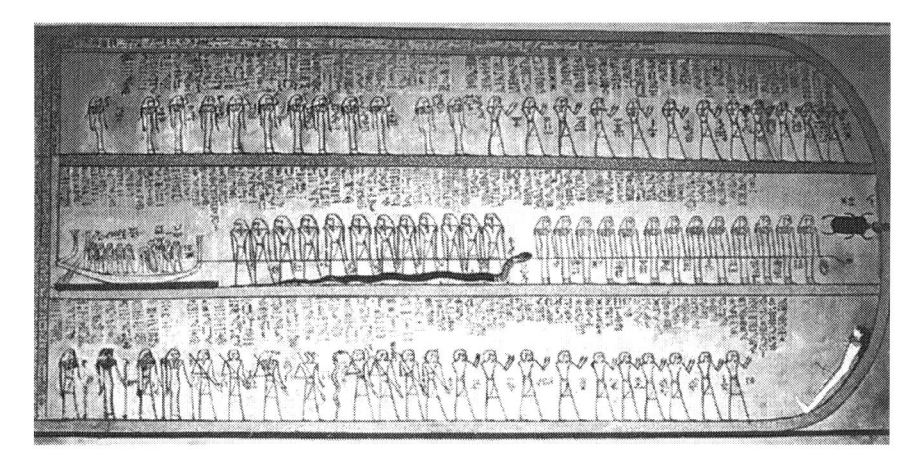

Detail of the decoration from the walls of the burial chamber of the tomb of Amenhotep II (KV-35).

This tomb was subject of an unfortunate incident a few years after its discovery. Contrary to the opinion of its discoverer, the

Egyptian authorities decided that some of the mummies were to be left in place where they were found. So when they finished the work of documentation and removal of material findings, the entrance was walled back up again leaving the bodies of Amenhotep II, the three mummies without bandages and the mummy lying on the boat. But in 1901 the looters returned to business. They entered the tomb and brought the king from his sarcophagus in search of the jewels they believed he still held. Finally, all they took was the boat on which rested the other mummy near the entrance, shattering the mummy in the process. Damages on the mummy of Amenhotep were not severe, but this incident showed that the mentality of some of the locals had changed little in the last three millennia.

Portrait of Victor Loret (1859, Paris-1946, Lyon), the discoverer of the tomb KV - 35.

Current View of the well that leads to the cachette of Bab el Gassus. As seen it is very close to the temples of Deir el Bahari.

153 Mummies Seek Refuge

We don't want to end this book without mentioning one last mummy hideout. This is the cachette of Bab el Gassus, discovered in 1891 by another Frenchman, Eugène Grebaut. The tomb is also located near Deir el-Bahari, and in it were found no less than 153 mummies dating from the XXI Dynasty; mostly priests and priestesses of Ammon accompanied by some of their relatives, including several children, but no pharaohs.

This tomb was accessed through an eleven foot deep hole, the bottom of which a gallery of 93 meters opened which flowed into two square burial chambers. Shortly before reaching the chambers, a transverse gallery of 60 meters was opened eastward, giving us a total length between the two tunnels of 153 meters.

It is believed that an earlier tomb was used as a base and extended for the specific purpose of hosting these mummies, which were moved there from their original graves during the reign of Psusennes II, the last pharaoh of the XXI Dynasty (about 950/940 B.C.)

Bab el Gasus Tomb

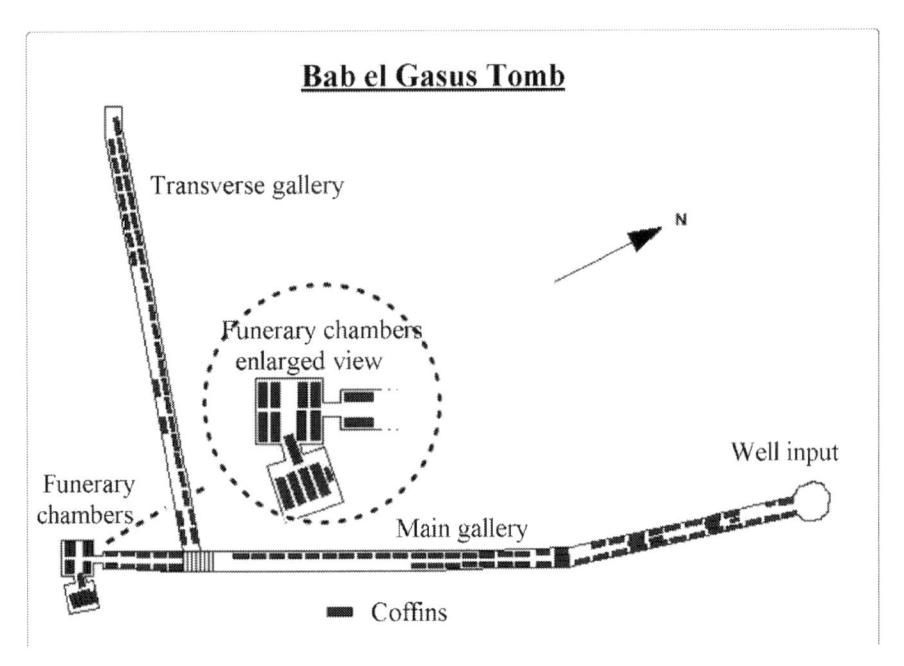

Plan of the *cachette* of Bab el Gassus, containing a total of 153 mummies of priests and priestesses of Ammon, accompanied by some of their relatives.

The tomb was found intact, with all the sarcophagi in good condition as well as important funerary equipment, and if Grebaut located it was thanks to the services of an old acquaintance of ours: Mohamed Abdel Rassul. While on an official excavation of another burial, his experience as a graverobber led him to question the mere soil characteristics of a nearby plot of land, and suspected there was a burial located there, as well. A probe then confirmed his suspicions, and the *cachette* was located.

Given this avalanche of mummies, coffins and grave goods, Egyptian authorities made a controversial decision. After selecting the best sarcophagi that remained in Cairo, they gave the rest to the countries that had sent representatives to the inauguration of the new viceroy of Egypt, Abbas II. Roughly similar lots were divided, of about four coffins each, plus grave goods, and then distributed out between those states, while all the mummies themselves were sent to the museum of Cairo. At first, some 17 museums were graced with the pieces, but over the years, the sets have been dispersed, and it is now possible to find objects of this tomb in dozens of collections around the world. To make matters worse, boxes and covers of many coffins were mixed together, and many mummies disappeared entirely. In a 1908 report, the Egyptologist George Daressy indicated that 60 mummies were lost shortly after arriving in Cairo. Today there are 93 mummies from the tomb that are missing.

Coffin that belonged to Asetemakhbit with part of his funerary equipment. It was one of those located in Bab el Gassus, and today is exposed in the National Archaeological Museum in Madrid.

Despite the disaster of this institutional looting, we can keep the positive aspect in mind that today it's at least possible to enjoy objects from this tomb in museums scattered around the world.

Bust of Queen Cleopatra VII. Her tomb is one of the most sought-after in Egyptian soil, but so far his whereabouts remain unknown. Royal Museum in Ontario (Canada)

Conclusion

The discovery of the *cachette* of the royal mummies of Deir el Bahari was a real earthquake in scientific fields of its time. On top of the unrivaled archaeological value of the find, it meant something even more important, the realization that there was still much to discover from Pharaonic Egypt, as there were many who at that time believed that the great discoveries had already come and gone.

As we have read, the continued possibilities of Egyptian antiquity was confirmed shortly after the discovery of the other two mummies hideouts we have discussed in this book, but also later on with the discovery in the twentieth century of the nearly intact tomb of Tutankhamun and the royal necropolis of Tanis, which included several non-violated tombs.

This leads us to believe that the findings have not finished in the lands of the Nile, there are many gaps in the royal lists that remain to be completed: we don't know the whereabouts of most of the kings of the dynasties XV and XVI, and of the queens of the XVIII dynasty; and the tombs and the mummies of Thutmose II, Ramesses VIII, Alexander the Great, and the *mediatic* couple of Queen Cleopatra and the Roman general Mark Antony, have yet to be discovered.

Despite the turbulent times that Egypt is experiencing right now, many teams of archaeologists, both Egyptian and from other countries, have not stopped working on the ground. Excavations continue on across the country, and at any moment the news could break of a great discovery that could –why not– overshadow every other discovery made so far.

Image from a British illustrated weekly newspaper dated in 1906, showing the uncovering of a tomb at Deir el Bahari.

SECOND BOOK

Tutankhamun's Tomb and the Curse of the Mummies

Solid gold mask that covered the head and shoulders of Pharaoh Tutankhamun. Undoubtedly the most famous piece of all that were contained in his tomb and an icon of ancient Egyptian culture.

First Part: Tutankhamun's Tomb

Introduction. The Start of an Amazing Adventure

—Can you see anything?

—Yes, wonderful things.

This brief dialogue between Lord Carnarvon and Howard Carter, at the moment the latter looked for the first time inside Tutankhamun's tomb after three thousand years of darkness, packages into those few words many years of work and quest. Hard work digging under the merciless Egyptian sun, and intense quest for the remains that this ancient civilization, daughter of the Nile, left scattered all over the country. A search that was soon redirected to a more specific task, the location of an elusive and almost unknown pharaoh, a king insignificant for many, but which became overnight the best known of the rulers of Egypt; and the discovery of his tomb in one of the biggest moments of world archaeology of all time, and certainly the most recognized by the public.

But to get to this great discovery, there was a need to walk a long road plagued by uncertainties, setbacks and moments of discouragement, surpassed only by the strong will to move forward and a combative character that distinguished Carter.

Watercolor painted by Howard Carter in 1896. The copy of the reliefs and paintings that covered the Egyptian monuments was what led Carter to the Land of the Nile in 1891. There he stood out for the quality of his work.

We can start our story well before that of November 26th, 1922, specifically in 1891. That year the young Carter, who had partly learned and partly inherited from his father a remarkable ability for drawing and painting, left his England homeland and traveled to Egypt at only 17 years-old, employed by the Egypt Exploration Fund through Egyptologist Percy Newberry to copy the reliefs and inscriptions of various monuments from Beni Hasan and El-Bersha. In fact, his first contact with Egyptian antiquities was somewhat earlier, as he had the opportunity to sketch the collection of a wealthy Norfolk landowner: Lord Amherst. Once in Egypt he was also able to work for a few years with eminent Egyptologists such as Flinders Petrie, who was excavating in El Amarna, or Edouard Neville, who did the same in Deir el Bahari. From them he learned the techniques of excavation, since Carter lacked any academic training related to archaeology or history, but also learned firsthand the management of human and material resources, which often caused more headaches than the excavations themselves.

Carter soon acquired prestige with his drawings, far superior in quality to those other colleagues were doing, since he was not limited to the tracing of the reliefs and paintings, but rather he copied them with impeccable technique.

His good work and the recommendation of Neville lead to Gaston Maspero, chief back then of the Egyptian Antiquities Service, to appoint him Inspector General of Monuments of Upper Egypt in 1899; a charge he exchanged in 1904 to the one of Inspector of Lower Egypt.

During his time in Deir el Bahari an episode that decisively influenced Carter's way of working took place. Once the area suffered a heavy storm, when he headed to the temple the next day to check the damage, his horse caught one of its legs within a hole in the sand. After inspecting Carter believed it to be a possible tomb, but it was outside his concession area, so he couldn't excavate it. When shortly after he got his position as inspector, he decided to excavate the site and, indeed, he found a tomb (which has since become known as the Tomb of the Horse) which had a sarcophagus, a statue wrapped in fabric and several containers. But, what really intrigued him was a closed shaft he considered would lead to an intact burial chamber. He organized an official opening attended by various authorities, but when they opened the shaft they only found some vases and votive boats. This gaffe made Carter become more cautious, as he would show in future actions.

From his new positions he worked in the research and protection of the rich Egyptian heritage, which caused him quite a few setbacks, such as accusations of favoritism and trade in antiquities. One of the major problems arose following the discovery of the tomb of Amenhotep II in the Valley of the Kings, made by French archaeologist Victor Loret in 1898. In the tomb there were twelve other mummies in addition to the original owner, and most were moved to the Cairo Museum but, by decision of Carter, Amenhotep's mummy was left in the tomb. In 1902 the tomb was robbed by thieves who mistakenly believed that the king still had his jewels. Luckily, though the mummy was removed from the coffin and thrown on the floor, it wasn't damaged. Still, this fact was used by some to criticize the Carter administration.

But the most serious incident was caused by a group of French tourists who, while drunk, had caused a scene by the Serapeum of Memphis and even confronted the guards who berated them for their attitude. Carter couldn't help but to side with the guards, to whom he even gave the green light to use force to defend against them. The rioter received some stick hits, but these tourists, with money and influence, demanded a formal apology at their consulate. Carter didn't apologize, and although his superiors trusted and sided with him, the situation continued escalating, until he finally resigned in 1905.

We see here how the whims of fate sometimes play an important role in the course of History. If some rude tourists hadn't mounted a scandal in the Serapeum, our guy would have continued his work in Sakkara, perhaps escalating to management positions of increasing responsibility, but instead he became jobless overnight, and with an uncertain future.

Instead of returning to Britain, Carter preferred to stay in Egypt, where his artistic skills allowed him to earn a living painting beautiful watercolors of monuments and landscapes which he sold to tourists. In addition, his contacts and knowledge allowed him to actively participate in the business of antiques, but his economic situation was far from buoyant.

Despite problems, Gaston Maspero continued appreciating that impetuous young man in whom he recognized ample virtues, so when a wealthy English nobleman appeared looking for someone to excavate for him, Maspero didn't hesitate to recommend Carter.

As you may have guessed, that British rich man was none other than Lord Carnarvon. His full name was George Edward Stanhope Molyneux Herbert, fifth Earl of Carnarvon, and at only 23 years-old he had inherited a huge fortune upon the death of his father. Like many in his position, one of his main problems was to find a way to fight the boredom of having life already solved from the cradle. But unlike most, our guy had other concerns; he had a passion for art and antiques, and since his years at the Trinity College in Cambridge he had already collected paintings and antique prints. He was a keen sportsman and skilled rider and celebrated receiving his heritage by sailing around the world in a sailboat.

Photograph of Lord Carnarvon and Howard Carter during their work in the Valley of the Kings.

In those years a sport was born that seduced him from the start: car races, which back then was a new fad suitable only for the rich, who were the only ones who could afford those expensive machines. He was also one of the first in his country to succumb to the charms of cars themselves. In fact, his car was the third of such vehicles that circulated on the roads of Britain under license. He was fascinated by speed, and it nearly cost him his life.

In 1901 his car overturned near the German spa Langenschwalbach while trying to avoid a stopped car on the road, and he got trapped underneath. His companion managed to free him, but the accident left life-long consequences. He underwent numerous surgeries to try to rebuild his battered bones, but the pain would accompany him until his death. His lungs were also damaged, so the cold, wet English weather caused him respiratory problems. Doctors recommended for him to spend winters somewhere with a warm, dry climate. He chose Egypt, and that decision changed his life, and the history of archaeology.

He arrived in Egypt for the first time in 1903. There he discovered the world of archaeological excavations and decided that he, too, would take part in that activity. On the one hand it would allow him to fill his time, so he could enjoy his passion for history and collecting antiques. Moreover, according to the Egyptian law of that time, what was found in excavations was divided fifty-fifty between the Egyptian administration and whoever was making the discovery, so this meant the activity could also become a profitable investment.

In the winter of 1906 he decides to start his own excavations, but only six weeks were needed for him to realize he didn't have the knowledge or experience to develop the activity. He sought advice from Maspero who recommended the young Carter, for which he still felt a lot of appreciation.

It is at this point that the fate of Lord Carnarvon and Howard Carter intersect and join, and together they enter into the history books.

Anthropomorphic coffin discovered during excavations that Carnarvon and Carter conducted between 1907 and 1911 in the necropolis of the nobles which extends on the west bank of the Nile, among the fields and cliffs of Thebes.

The First Excavations

On the advice of Carter, our particular *dream team* began its excavations in the vicinity of Gurna. This village was built on the west bank of the Nile, literally on the ancient necropolis of the nobles. A gigantic city of the dead that villagers had been looting for centuries without scruple, and on which they had built their ruinous homes on top of the tombs.

Between 1907 and 1911 they excavated in this vast cemetery, where they made some interesting discoveries, collected all in Carnarvon's work *"Five Years' Exploration at Thebes."*

After these campaigns they completely changed the excavation area and moved to Sakha (formerly Xois) in the Nile Delta, but their luck changed, because after not even a month into the expedition, they had to abandon their work due to an invasion of cobras and horned vipers that made it impossible.

But Carter's obsession from long ago was to excavate in the Valley of the Kings. This valley, known in Arabic as Biban al Muluk (Kings' Gate), is in an inhospitable place behind the cliffs lining the Nile Valley, and consists of several *wadis* or dry creeks surrounded by high mountains that were reached by a narrow path. The first king we know for sure that was buried there was Thutmose I (1504 -1492 BC), although it is quite possible that his predecessor, Amenofis I, was already buried in the Valley; and it continued being used by most of the pharaohs of dynasties XVIII, XIX and XX.

Already in his years as Inspector of Upper Egypt, Carter was involved in the discovery and monitoring of the excavation of a pair of royal tombs for Theodore Davis, a lawyer and wealthy American businessman who funded the excavations and who still held the concession, although his patience began to run out, convinced that there was nothing else to be discovered in the valley. That very idea that in the Valley of the Kings all tombs had already been discovered had been exposed a century before by Giovanni Belzoni, Italian adventurer specializing in impossible missions, who had located and excavated four royal tombs there, and that as much as he searched wasn't able to find another one. After him came others such as British consul Henry Salt, or Richard Lepsius, who in-front of an imposing Prussian mission, measured and combed the valley without any results. Even so, after him arrived Victor Loret first, then Theodore Davis, who found new tombs before it became the turn of our men.

And so Howard Carter was convinced that the valley hadn't yet shown all its secrets. Even more, he believed that the last excavator,

Davis, was ignoring clear indications of the presence of an undiscovered tomb. That tomb was that of a minor and little known pharaoh who reigned for a few years: Tutankhamun.

But what made him think that the tomb of this king was waiting for his arrival? Four were the elements that induced Carter to believe that Tut's tomb was still in the valley, also in a very specific area, and the four had been found—and overlooked—by Davis' team.

In the last days of his excavations in the Valley, Davis had found hidden under a rock: a cup with the name of Tutankhamun and very near from there, a pit tomb containing an unidentified statue of alabaster and the remains of a wooden box, among which were pieces of gold foil with the name of Tutankhamun, his wife and that of his successor: Ay. Davis thought he had discovered the tomb of Tutankhamun and so he announced it, but this was, obviously, an improper burial for a pharaoh of the eighteenth dynasty, no matter how insignificant he would have been.

In 1907, Davis' team had located a tomb in the Valley—the KV-55—with a mixture of objects apparently belonging to the grave goods of several people. Among these were several clay seals with the name of Tutankhamun. Besides these pieces appeared a mummy that was rightly identified as that of Akhenaten, known as the "heretic pharaoh". That king, who according to DNA testing in 2010, would be Tut's father, had been moved from his original point of rest in El Amarna to KV-55, most likely by his son.

But the most significant finding was produced during that same campaign of 1907-1908. Back then Davis' operatives had located hidden in an unfinished tomb carved into the rock, a dozen large ceramic vessels with hieratic inscriptions on the sides and sealed mouths. Davis was disappointed when they opened them and found inside nothing more than pieces of linen, lots of ceramic fragments, animal bones, bags with natron and some other items that were not part of any grave goods, so he abandoned them in a warehouse without giving them greater importance.

But some time later, the American Egyptologist Herbert E. Winlock saw the vessels and considered that they warranted a more detailed study. With Davis' permission, he sent them to the Metropolitan Museum of New York. There, it was confirmed the importance of the find, as the conclusion reached by researchers was that the shawls and linen bandages, flower pendant, remains of pottery vessels, food, natron, etc., were nothing less than the elements used in embalming and funeral ceremonies and banquets held in honor of a king, and that king was none other than Tutankhamun, whose name appeared in several clay seals that were also part of the collection.

So we have four clues: the cup under the stone, the box with gold leaf, clay seals from Akhenaten's tomb and the vessels with the remains of the funeral ceremonies, and all were located in the same area in the center of the Valley. Carter was convinced that Tutankhamun's tomb could not be far behind.

Finally, in 1914 came the long-awaited news: Davis had given up the concession for the Valley of the Kings, convinced that there was nothing left to discover. Carnarvon took it and began planning work with Carter, who proposed to excavate a triangular area between the tombs of Ramses II, Merneptah and Ramses VI, which occupied about one hectare.

The outbreak of the First World War after a few months into the dig paralyzed work as Carnarvon had to return to England, the workers were recruited by the army, and Carter had to perform work for the government as a member of the Military Intelligence Service. The work was not resumed in the Valley until 1917.

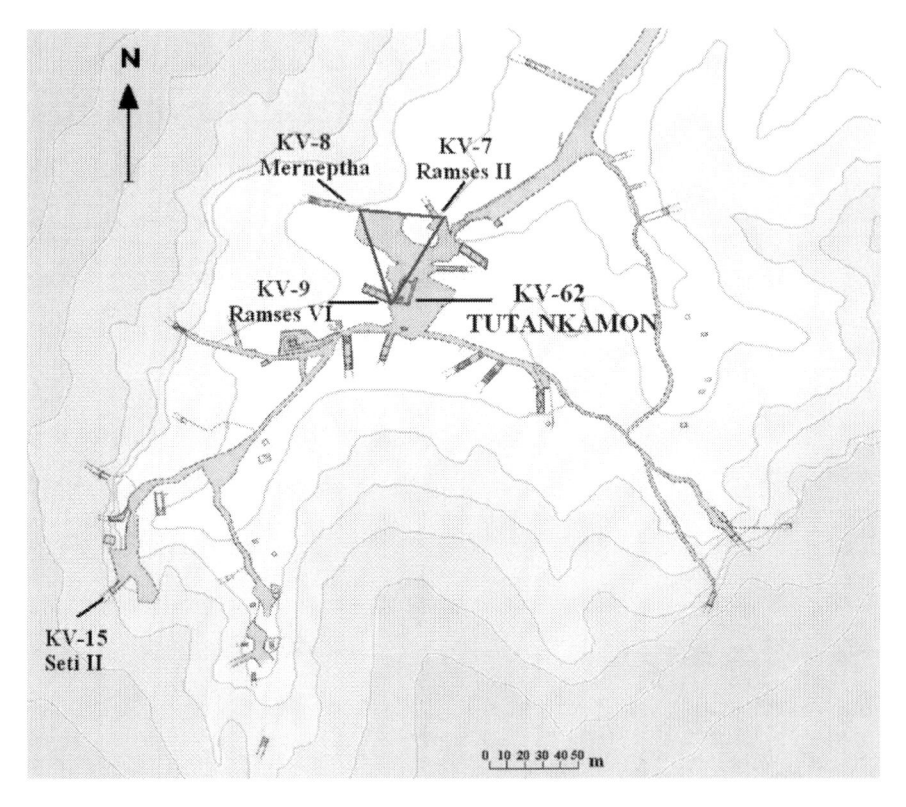

Map of the Valley of the Kings, with the triangle that Carter and Carnarvon marked and in which they believed they could find the tomb of Tutankhamun. As can be seen, this triangle barely scratches the entrance to the tomb, so they were close to not finding it. It has also marked tomb KV-15, where they installed the warehouse and restoration workshop. Drawing from the author.

The main problem they faced to begin their work was that at that time, after countless excavation campaigns by more or less professional teams, the whole valley seemed like a real battlefield, full of holes and piles of rubble, and so it was literally impossible to know which areas were excavated and which were not. There was only one solution, and that was to clean the entire surface of the chosen area, reaching down to the bedrock. Any openings would then remain to be seen. But of course, that was something easier said than done, as many tons of earth and piled stones had to be removed. To expedite the work they decided to use rail wagons to evacuate the large amount of debris well away from the working area.

Despite the difficulties, in the first year an important part of the area was cleared, reaching the door of the tomb of Ramses VI, of the Twentieth Dynasty, where were found the remains of huts that had been erected by the workers who dug that tomb. The cabins were built with large siles boulders, material that in this place meant the closeness of a tomb. Since Ramses VI's was one of the most visited tombs of the valley and the excavation of the cabins would cut off access to it, they decided to postpone that excavation. A mistake that almost cost them the loss of the discovery.

In the 1919/20 campaign they got to clear and explore the whole triangle except the workers' huts, and although they found no tomb, they did find a cache containing thirteen alabaster jars with the names of Ramses II and Merneptah. It wasn't what they were searching for, but it was still a great find, so much that the daughter of Lord Carnarvon (Lady Evelin) herself insisted on digging them up themselves with their own hands.

The next campaign was devoted to digging a small side valley where the tomb of Thutmose II was found, with rather poor results. The 1921/22 campaign was delayed by health problems of Carter, who had surgery on the gallbladder, so the excavation of the huts was postponed for the next campaign.

Time passed, and the findings didn't come. Lord Carnarvon began to lose patience when noticing his money vanished without getting anything in return, and there came a time when he openly raised to Carter that perhaps others were right and there was nothing left to discover. It was time to leave the Valley.

But Carter refused to leave, not until exploring every corner of that triangle, which was magical for him, where he was convinced that the boy king awaited them, sleeping his dreams for centuries. They had been digging for five years yes, but in reality there had been only eight months of effective work. It was not much. Given the refusal of Carnarvon, Carter even offered to make a final excavation campaign paying for it out of his own pocket.

Moved by the archaeologist's blind trust, Lord Carnarvon relented and granted him one last chance. If they found nothing in that winter they would leave the Valley definitely.

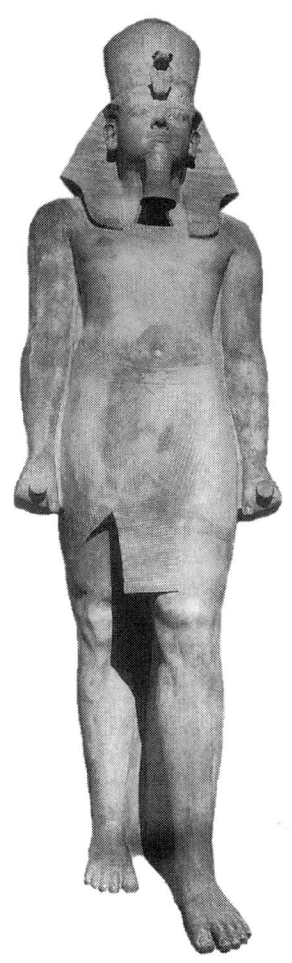

Colossal sculpture representing King Tutankhamun from Medinet Abu, and that today is exhibited in the Museum of Oriental Institute in Illinois (USA). Most of the young king's sculptures were later usurped by his successors, mainly Horemheb.

But, who was Tutankhamun?

It is somewhat curious that the best known pharaoh to the general public is a historically insignificant king who had no time to make significant events during his short reign.

When we try to know the details of the reign of our hero, we encounter a dual problem. The usual difficulty of obtaining information about events that occurred more than three thousand years ago joins the fact that there was a deliberate attempt to erase this particular period of Egyptian history for a long time. Temples and palaces were taken apart, inscriptions were erased and statues were destroyed or usurped.

Today we know that Tutankhamun (1336/5 to 1327/5 BC) was son of the "heretic king" Amenhotep IV (Akhenaten), who conducted a religious revolution in Egypt in which he closed the ancient temples and established the cult to a single god, Aten, the sun disk. He also built a new capital which he called Akhetaten at a place known today as Tell el Amarna. These two actions reduced the power and income of the priests of Amun at Thebes drastically, which threatened the king with many powerful enemies.

Following the new doctrine, our protagonist received the name Tutankhaten at birth (Neb-Ra jeperu-Tut-ankh-Aten), which means Live Image of Aten.

We do not know the name of Tut's mother, although we have her mummy, located in 1898 in the tomb of Amenhotep II, and we know that she was also the sister of Akhenaten, which meant the young king was the son of an incestuous relationship. His grandparents were Amenhotep III and Queen Tiye.

Although this period of Egyptian history is one of the most obscure and difficult to document, it appears that during his last years of life, Akhenaten was accompanied by a regent named Nefernefruaton, which for some was none other than his wife Nefertiti. After the death of the "Heretic King" and the brief reign of Nefernefruaton with a consort of the name Smenkare (they ruled just for a year), Tutankhaten came to the throne when he was only nine years old, so the one whom really ruled Egypt was the Grand Vizier Ay and Horemheb, who among other positions of importance was the army chief. Both would come to reign years later.

The boy king married Princess Ankhesenpaaten, third daughter of Akhenaten and Nefertiti.

In a block of stone reused in Amarna there is a surprising inscription. According to this, the eleven year old Ankhesenpaaten would have had a daughter of his father Akhenaten, with whom she would have married earlier. If this inscription is correct, we see how Tutankhamun married his half-sister who at the same time was his widowed stepmother.

The most notable achievement of the reign of our protagonist was that when he hadn't yet been two years on the throne, he returned Egypt to religious orthodoxy, returning to the priests of Amun the power that had been snatched from them by his father and so he moved the royal court back to Thebes. Consistent with this political-religious turn, he changed his name to Tutankhamun (Live Image of Amun), as did his wife, who was renamed Ankhesenamun.

His death befell after ten years of his reign, when he was only nineteen years old, and was totally unexpected, as it's clear from the characteristics of the tomb, much more appropriate for a noble than for a king. There are some researchers who are convinced that the tomb where he was buried was actually excavated for his vizier Ay. On the possible causes of his death we will talk further below.

When he died he was childless, and was succeeded by his

former vizier Ay, who married the widowed queen Ankhesenamun. After only four years of reign Ay died too, leaving the throne to the former general Horemheb. The latter was quick to erase all traces of the boy king from monuments and substituting Tut's name for his own, a way of reaffirming that it was actually he who had built them and who had ruled from the shade.

In the Hittite archives we find an exceptional document. A letter possibly sent by Ankhesenamun in which she announced to king Subbiluliuma that she had been widowed and desperate, asking him to send one of his sons to marry her:

"My husband has died and I have no son. They say that you have many sons. You might give me one of your sons to become my husband. I would not wish to take one of my subjects as a husband... I am afraid".

The king was puzzled by the letter from the queen of a country considered an enemy, so he asked for clarification. The widow reiterated the request, insisting on the offer to make one of his sons into the king of Egypt, and so prince Zannanza left immediately for the country of the Nile, although he never reached his destination. Presumably both Ay and Horemheb knew about the content of the letters, and spies would have been placed on the border to prevent at all costs the Hittite prince from meeting with Ankhesenamun. There was much that was at stake, nothing less than the throne of Egypt.

To end this chapter we include a fact that has greatly surprised researchers, and it is that genetic studies performed in 2010 to a group of mummies, among which was that of Tutankhamun, in addition to revealing the identities of their immediate families, have contributed some curious facts, such as that the king belonged to a genetic profile known as haplogroup R1b1a2, which is shared by 70% of the current Spanish and British male population, while in the whole of Europe, males carrying the same profile account for 50%.

But most striking is that in his home country, Egypt, only one percent of the current population has it. This seems to indicate that the ancestors of King Tut came from somewhere other than the country of the Nile. In particular, experts believe that most likely the common ancestor lived in the Caucasus 9,500 years ago.

Old photograph of the Valley of the Kings. The various wadis and canyons that converge in the central valley can be perfectly seen.

The Discovery of the Tomb

Carter arrived to Luxor on October 22nd, 1922 for his last campaign in the Valley of the Kings. His situation was delicate, so there was no time to lose. He placed his team to work and by November 3rd they had already brought to light many of the stone huts that stretched in-front of the tomb of Ramses VI whose excavation had been delayed for six campaigns. Once they studied them and built a plan of their exact layout, they demolished them in-order to dig the meter of soil that remained under them. This would continue until they reached bare rock, which was scheduled for the next day's work.

When Carter returned in the morning he was surprised by the silence in the excavation. Neither the rhythmic pounding of the tools nor the songs with which workers accompanied them could be heard.

Why had the workers stopped? Someone came running. A step carved on the rock had appeared just below the first cabin they had demolished.

He rushed to the site, inspected the pit and ordered them to resume work immediately. The first step was followed by a second and a third, and a fourth ... Just four meters below the entrance to the tomb of Ramses VI they kept digging a deep cut in the rock leaving an opening of a very well-known type in the Valley. It was clear that it was the entrance to a tomb and that, since on it had been built huts during the twentieth dynasty, it was evident not only that this tomb was prior to that time, but had not been the victim of a subsequent looting that occurred especially during the XXI Dynasty, when tomb robberies were generalized and even institutionalized.

They kept digging all day, unearthing what was a downward passage three meters high and just under two wide. When the last rays of sun disappeared behind the cliffs that closed the Valley, at the level of the twelfth step, there appeared the top of a sealed door that showed the seals of the royal necropolis—a jackal on top of nine kneeling captives. That meant they were at the tomb of a dignitary or perhaps a king. Although the fact that the entrance was much smaller than that of the royal tombs they knew averted a little bit of this possibility.

Carter made a small hole in the wall and introduced a flashlight through it. Behind the wall, debris filled the corridor to the ceiling, which seemed further proof that the tomb was intact. But it was getting dark and they had to leave it. In addition, Lord Carnarvon was in England, so Carter had to make a very difficult decision for him.

Overcoming his first impulses he ordered to cover back up the hole in the door. Whatever it was that awaited them behind that door, it was deserving that whoever had staked his heritage was present at the discovery.

A few centimeters below where they stopped digging that day there appeared, clearly visible, the stamps with the name of Tutankhamun. If they had dug a little more, Carter would have been spared the doubts that were assaulting him during the weeks of waiting, not knowing to whom the tomb could belong to.

Photos from the entrance to the tomb of Tutankhamun, which is now known as KV 62 (King Valley-62). As we see the photo on the left was taken after it was covered while waiting for the arrival of Lord Carnarvon.

He left his most trusted men on guard and exultantly, rode down the valley toward his home. In the morning, the first thing he did was send a telegram to Lord Carnarvon:

"At last have made wonderful discovery in valley; a magnificent tomb with seals intact; re-covered same for your arrival; congratulations."

He then returned to the Valley. He had to secure the tomb until Carnarvon's arrival. He returned to fill the gap, dug up the ground and set on top the large blocks of stone with which the demolished workers' huts had been built.

Two days after the discovery word had already gotten out and he began to get compliments and offers of help. Carnarvon also answered on day eight with two telegrams: "Possibly I will go soon" and "I propose to reach Alexandria on the 20th".

Carter spent the two weeks before the arrival of his sponsor to make the necessary preparations before his arrival. Thus, when on November 22 Lord Carnarvon landed with his daughter Evelin, they had already removed the debris that was piled over the entrance to the tomb, so they could go straight to cleaning the stairs.

On the 24th the 16 steps were clean and they could see in daylight the walled up door in its entirety. Then the first disappointment arrived. There were two unmistakable intrusion marks. Twice had they pierced the wall, although it was true that on both occasions they had recovered the holes with the seals of the Royal Necropolis. That meant that, almost certainly, the tomb had not been completely ransacked.

They brought down the door and for two days cleaned the descending passage of debris until ten meters below there appeared a walled door similar to the first, with the same royal seals in the plaster and the same traces of intrusion covered again. It was November 26th, 1922. A day that would mark the annals of the history of archaeology.

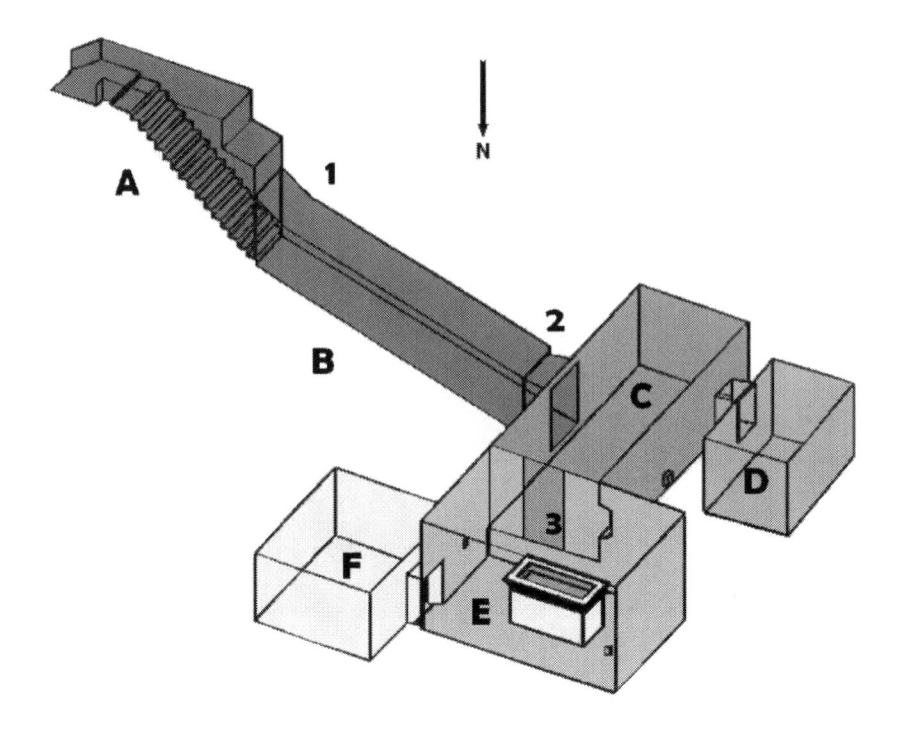

Plan of Tutankhamen's Tomb. A: entrance staircase; B: descending passage; C: antechamber; D: annex; E: burial chamber with sarcophagus; F: treasure; 1: first door boarded-up; 2: second door boarded-up; 3: Sealed door of the burial chamber. Drawing from the author.

They didn't want to raise their hopes too much, as during the excavation of the aisle they had found traces of grave goods with the names of several different pharaohs, so it was quite possible that they were facing not a real tomb, but a cache of mummies similar to ones they'd found before. Soon, however, they would clear their doubts.

Carter made a small hole in the upper left corner and introduced an iron bar. He moved it. On the other side there was no more debris or stones, nothing but air. He then placed a candle beside the hole to check that the air was not contaminated, and then he widened the opening a little, introduced the candle through it and peered in.

Behind him, Lord Carnarvon, Lady Evelyn and Egyptologist Arthur Callender, who had been helping Carter from the moment of the discovery, held their breathes.

Carter wouldn't say a word. This is what he would tell us later:

"At first I could see nothing, the hot air escaping from the chamber causing the candle flame to flicker, but presently, as my eyes grew accustomed to the light, details of the room within emerged slowly from the mist, strange animals, statues, and gold - everywhere the glint of gold. For the moment - an eternity it must have seemed to the others standing by - I was struck dumb with amazement, and when Lord Carnarvon, unable to stand the suspense any longer, inquired anxiously, 'Can you see anything?' it was all I could do to get out the words, 'Yes, wonderful things".

View of the north-side of the antechamber. In the background the two life-size sculptures guarding the walled entrance to the burial chamber can be seen. At the bottom we can observe the lid of a basket above some reeds that possibly covered the hole made by Carter to check the contents of the chamber.

A Colossal Work

After demolishing the sealed door, they could see that the wonderful objects glimpsed by Carter were piled everywhere, filling the room known since then as the antechamber. To their left, parts of disassembled chariots piled up, while in-front of them they could distinguish huge beds with animal heads, boxes and chests, vases of numerous forms, many egg-shaped boxes, bows, canes... and altogether more than 600 objects, but when they recovered from the initial shock they realized that there was no trace of coffins or sarcophagi anywhere. Where was the mummy?

They soon discovered that at the bottom there were two life-size wooden statues facing each other, and between them they could perfectly see another door boarded up and sealed. Certainly, the king would be resting there, and who knows with what riches. Or perhaps what awaited them on the other side of the wall was another room equal to the one they were seeing, or many? ... Their imaginations flew unbridled, and after seeing what was before them, they could no longer put limits on their thoughts. Everything was possible. And even more when they discovered under one of the beds located opposite to the entrance, a small hole that gave way to another small room (known as the annex) full of objects crowded into a chaotic clutter, undoubtedly caused by thieves.

In addition to the rich objects, those present were excited to see much simpler details that provided a more human dimension to their discovery. In the dust of the ground they could still see the imprint of the bare foot of a worker, the second door showed the imprints of the fingers of the workers, and beside it stood still the bucket with mortar which had been used to seal it.

The next day the official visit took place by the local inspector of antiquities, and from the outset it was decided not to touch nor move anything until each object was perfectly recorded and photographed in its original position. And, although the waiting would be hard, the sealed door between the statues would not be opened until the antechamber was completely emptied.

They were facing a huge task never done before, they had to prepare everything thoroughly and that took time, so on December 3, as a preemptive measure to avoid surprises; Carter and Carnarvon decided, very wisely, to re-cover the entrance again with earth. They couldn't risk that while they were making preparations, grave robbers would return to act as they did so many times before.

Carnarvon had to return to England, and Carter traveled to Cairo, where one of the first things he did was to commission an iron fence that would be placed on the inner door as complement to the wooden one that was already closing the outer door. He also provisioned for all the equipment he felt they could need: a car, photographic equipment, chemicals, packaging boxes of various types and sizes, thirty-three calico bales, over a kilometer and a half of wadding and a lot of bandages.

In this photo we can see most of the team that carried out the study of the contents of the tomb. From left to right: Arthur Mace, Richard Bethell, Arthur Callender, Lady Evelin Herbert, Howard Carter, Lord Carnarvon, Alfred Lucas and Harry Burton.

They knew the work that awaited them was immense and were aware that it would be impossible to be carried out by the two of them. They had to assemble a suitable team, and from the outset the international scientific community responded, as they had never done before and totally selflessly, in the request for help from our men. They were facing one of the greatest archaeological discoveries of all time, and everyone wanted to be there, to see it for themselves and participate in the success in one way or another.

Two of the first to join the team were Egyptologist Arthur Mace and Harry Burton, a photographer to whom we owe all those wonderful photos of the tomb and its contents that have been reproduced so many times. Both were in Thebes at the time with an expedition of the Metropolitan Museum in New York.

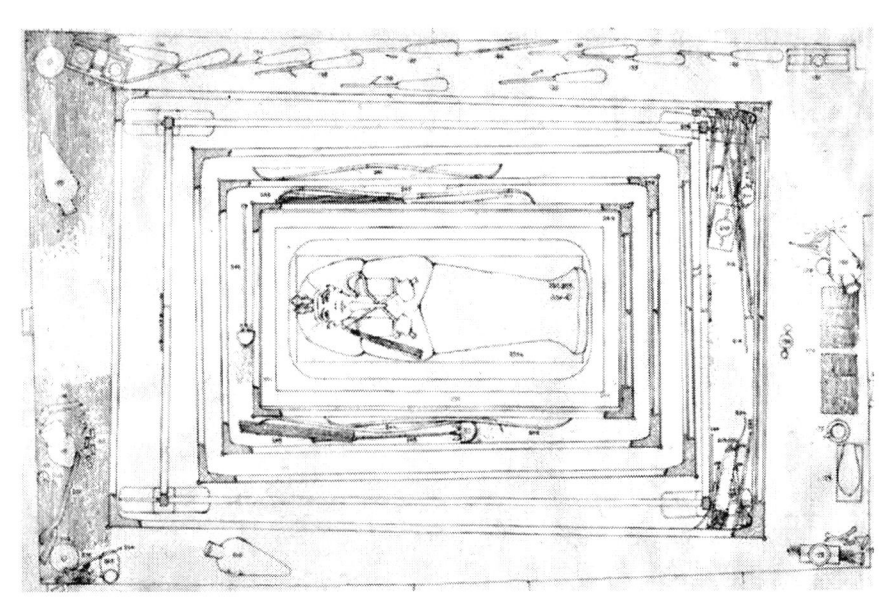

All the pieces found were photographed by H. Burton and drawn by F. Hall and W. Hauser before moving them. Drawing of the sarcophagi, chapels and objects around them.

Other specialists that joined were artists Lindley F. Hall and Walter F. Hauser, Alan Gardiner, who would be responsible for the inscriptions, chemist Alfred Lucas, and Percy E. Newberry, who examined the plants and flowers that formed the many necklaces and bouquets they found, and that by studying the growing and flowering season of each species, was able to determine that the burial of Tutankhamun took place between March and April. Carter often leaned on Arthur Callender as his confidant.

They also needed suitable places for specialists to develop their work, but the problem was that they were in the middle of nowhere, without any buildings in a kilometer radius. So, they decided to use some of the tombs in the necropolis.

As photo lab they used a small unmarked grave next to Akhenaten's, while they decided that of Seti II (KV-15) would be used as a warehouse and restoration workshop because, although it was distant from Tut's tomb, it provided security, adequate space and, above all, peace.

On December 16th, once everything was ready, the tomb was reopened and the work began. An effective work system was established in a way that was simple but orderly: First, Burton took the photographs of objects, which had previously been labeled with a number, then Hall and Hauser sketched them in their exact site placing them on a scaled plane, then Carter and Callender took some notes and the artefacts were transferred to the laboratory, where Mace and Lucas were responsible for the consolidation and conservation treatments and proceeded to creating a more detailed description of the item.

The accumulation and stacking of pieces was such that the movement of one could cause the one laying on it to fall. To prevent disaster, they devised a system of small scaffolding and props to fasten objects while others were removed. The situation in the annex was even more chaotic, so that when the time came to work there they used another method. Through a system of guides and pulleys, workers were suspended in the air above the items, so they could manipulate them without having to set foot on the ground.

The tomb's security was an obsession for Carnarvon and Carter (recall the incident with the mummy of Amenhotep II), so an ingenious method of monitoring was organized in which three separate groups took part that controlled each other and responded to different managers. In addition, we already said that even before the opening of the first gate, Carter had ordered a heavy wooden gate to secure the tomb early on.

Tutankhamun's tomb soon became a tourist destination, and every day a large number of journalists and onlookers swirled to the doors hoping to see a piece coming out.

On the 18th Burton took the first photographs of the antechamber and on the 27th he removed the first object of the burial, an extraordinary wooden casket decorated with elaborately painted scenes and containing clothes, shoes and other personal belongings of the pharaoh.

To transport the pieces safely and comfortably a multitude of wooden stretchers were built with added quilting, and the objects were set upon them with bandages to prevent their movement.

The exiting of the workers from the tomb, carrying items, was the most anticipated moment by many tourists, journalists and onlookers who crowded at the entrance to the tomb. Generally, once a day a delegation escorted by the military moved the stretchers loaded with the recovered items to the tomb that served as the object restoration workshop and warehouse. The cameras didn't stop shooting while reporters took notes and visitors pointed to the wonderful pieces until they moved out of sight.

During work on the tomb they soon found the traces left by thieves. Although the antechamber was in a relative order, they immediately realized that this order wasn't real, but someone had hastily relocated parts after the intrusion was discovered. The objects had been introduced into boxes and chests that were not theirs, and fallen pieces had been placed standing. The room known as the annex was just as the thieves had left it, and presumably likewise they would have left the antechamber as well. Later they discovered that they had also entered the burial chamber and the room known as "the treasury", here the effects of the visit were less visible, but there's clear evidence that many valuable pieces are missing, especially jewels.

Everything indicates that there were two attempted robberies, and that at first the descending passage between the two sealed doors was empty, as remains of broken items appeared on the floor. The evidence suggests that the dozen vessels found by Davis in 1908 and that finally ended up containing the elements used during Tutankhamun's mummification and funerary feast were originally deposited in this corridor, but after the first intrusion by the thieves, they were moved to where they were eventually found in order to fill the hall with earth and stones in an attempt to hinder subsequent entries, although the second intrusion couldn't be prevented.

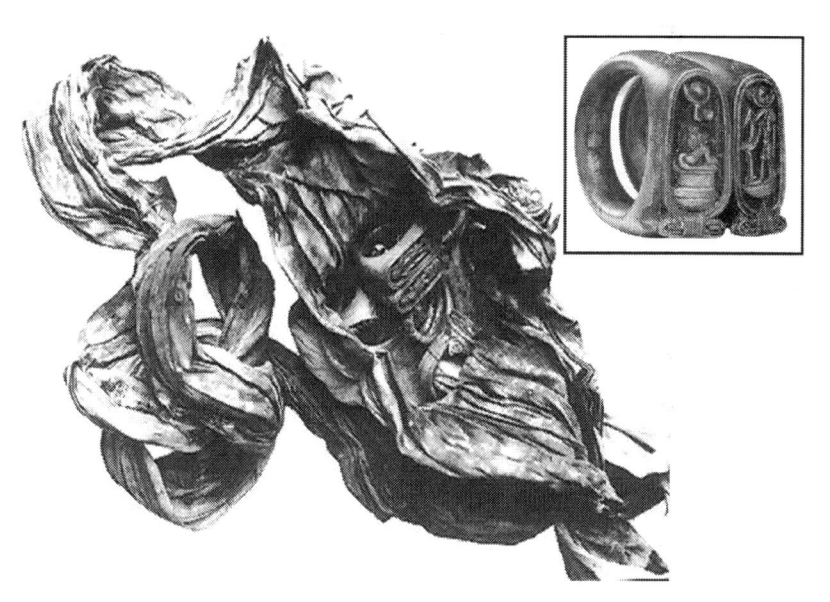

This piece of cloth was actually a shawl belonging to the king, and contained several gold rings. Surely it was used by thieves to wear the jewelry attached to their bodies in case they had to flee, leaving the remaining more difficult to transport objects. The fact that it was found in the grave suggests that at least some of the thieves were arrested. Detail of one of the rings it contained.

There is evidence to suggest that, at least on one occasion, the thieves were caught inside the tomb or as they fled with the loot. The most obvious is a small package made out of a shawl from the king, containing a handful of gold rings. Surely the shawl would have been used by one of the thieves to carry the rings strapped to his body in case he had to flee and leave the rest of the loot. These rings were reintegrated into a box they didn't belong to, something we know because there is a list of the objects contained in the top of many of the boxes. Such lists were used to facilitate the preparation of the inventory of the grave, and had also allowed the archeologists to know of the existence of many of the objects that had disappeared.

We see how, despite the efforts of the authorities from Pharaonic times, it was very difficult to stop the robberies in the tombs, as the accumulated treasures inside were a very attractive booty to a starving population, even though everyone knew that if they were caught they could expect one of the most terrible deaths ever devised by man: impalement.

Work on the grave continued relentlessly and by mid-February of 1923, after seven weeks of intense work, the antechamber was completely evacuated, but they had to wait until May 13 for the first thirty-four boxes to be transferred to Cairo. For that they used wagons that sled above movable rails, and because there was not enough railing to cover the 1500 meters that had to be covered to reach the Nile, they dismantled the sections already used in order to reassemble them later ahead.

On February 17th, around twenty people chosen among authorities and scientists filled the antechamber to witness the solemn opening of the burial chamber. Everyone wondered what was waiting for them behind the sealed door. Well, not everybody, as it seems that Carter, Carnarvon and his daughter Evelin had already crossed it some time prior. They couldn't stand the wait, so they had carved out a hole in the base of the wall, through which they could penetrate inside and be the first to discover what was hidden in the tomb's inner sanctum.

That would explain something that has always struck me in old photographs of the tomb, the fact that almost the last thing that was removed from the antechamber were a lot of reeds and the top of a basket that rested on the boarded up door, and which actually disguised the hole made by their furtive incursion. Although Carter never publicly admitted this, Lucas acknowledged years later that Carter had confessed this to him. Furthermore, in a letter dated December 26th, 1922, i.e., almost two months before the official opening of the burial chamber, Lady Evelin thanks Carter that he had allowed her to get in there, adding that "that was the greatest moment of my life". It should be recalled here the disappointment of Carter when he arranged the official opening of the "Tomb of the Horse" years before. It was clear he didn't want to make a fool of himself again.

When, in-front of his distinguished audience, Carter removed the stones from the top row with extreme caution, there appeared what at first seemed like a wall of solid gold that occupied the entire visible width. He continued dismantling the wall until two hours later, they were able to access the chamber and check that what they had before them was not a wall of gold but a masterpiece of Egyptian handcrafts: a huge wooden chapel covered with gold and blue faience ornaments.

The burial chamber was the only room of the tomb with walls decorated with painted scenes. Carefully they surrounded the chapel along the narrow passage of about 65 cm that was between it and the wall. On the floor there were numerous offerings, and also they found out that there was still a last room that opened on the east wall, called "the treasury".

Entrance to the so-called "treasury" with the sculpture of the jackal god Anubis protecting the access. Behind we can see the chapel that held the canopic coffins containing the mummified viscera of the king.

This room contained some of the most beautiful objects from the tomb, and the entrance was "guarded" by a sculpture of the jackal god Anubis, lying on a podium shaped like a pylon and covered by a cloth. Behind it, some sort of golden chapel with its four faces protected by many sculptures of goddesses with their arms extended, and that Carter described as *"the most beautiful monument that I have ever seen, so lovely that it made one gasp with wonder and admiration."* Inside, a chest of alabaster stored into four compartments the embalmed viscera of the king, each within a small golden sarcophagus. Around the chapel, an enormous number of coffers and model ships filled the space.

Some of these boxes and caskets contained jewelry, but researchers concluded that many had been stolen. Specifically Carter believed that what they found represented less than 40 percent of the total jewelry deposited in the grave. Remains of theft appeared throughout the tomb, for example, in the narrow corridor that was in the burial chamber were the parts of two wide gold necklaces that thieves lost during their headlong flight.

Other findings from this room attracted the attention of archaeologists. In a box appeared two small wooden sarcophagi and inside them tiny mummies that were found to belong to two female fetuses, one of about seven months and the other somewhat younger. DNA analysis indicated that one of them is the daughter of Tutankhamun with total confidence, while there are very high chances that the other is a second child.

Also appeared another set of four anthropoid miniature coffins embedded one into the other. The third one contained a mummiform figurine of solid gold and a fourth coffin of only thirteen centimeters in length with the name of Queen Tiye on the outside. Inside, a strand of hair was kept that surely Tutankhamun kept in memory of his grandmother.

To avoid the temptation to enter the treasury and cause any of the artifacts to get misplaced or lost, the entrance was covered with planks until they finished the job with the chapel and the sarcophagus.

The first of the four chapels that enclosed the king's sarcophagus was open, but the rest kept the royal seals intact, indicating that the thieves didn't get there. Detail of one of these seals.

Going back to the burial chamber, during the previous inspection of the huge chapel that occupied the chamber, archaeologists discovered that the doors were locked with a deadbolt, but there were no seals on it. Had thieves gotten to it first? Carter unbolted the lock and opened the door, which made a creaking whine after more than three millennia of waiting. Inside they found another chapel enclosed by doors similar to the previous ones, but a detail made them take a calm breath; the lock wasn't damaged and the strings with the seal of the royal necropolis kept the doors closed. Thieves hadn't had the time to enter.

They decided to end the exploration for that day. *"We were in the presence of the dead king and had to show reverence." Carter said.*

Finally, there were four successive chapels that enclosed the sarcophagus, and they invested the entire next campaign in its opening and dissembling. To remove them they had to tear down the wall that separated the burial chamber from the antechamber, and yet the work was extremely difficult, because the pieces were huge and some weighed nearly a ton.

They were able to see first-hand the skill of the craftsmen who built them, but also the haste with which the burial occurred. Some sides of the chapels had been mounted upside down, so they didn't fit well. Even workers had to use the mallet in some places so that the assembly could be completed on time, with the décor being damaged as a result.

Finally, on February 3rd, 1924 they completely exposed the magnificent sarcophagus, carved from a single block of yellow quartzite 2.75 m long 1.47 wide and 1.47 high, completely covered with immaculate reliefs.

The lid, however, didn't have the same quality in craftsmanship as the sarcophagus. It was carved in pink granite, and they had died it to prevent it from being too out of tune with the whole. Furthermore, it was broken from its central part, although the crack had been filled with some sort of adhesive and then painted. Presumably due to some last minute unforeseen circumstance, they had to use this lid that had a lower quality than the sarcophagus. Perhaps the original broke or was not ready in time for the burial.

As was done with the opening of the burial chamber, the opening ceremony of the sarcophagus brought about a convening in the tomb of local authorities and renowned scientists.

Slowly, and through a system of pulleys, the heavy lid of about 1250 kg of weight was lifted and left a clear sight of the first of the golden coffins guarding the pharaoh's remains. It was covered with linen bandages, but when removing them they found that the whole coffin was decorated with a fine bas-relief, except for the head and hands, in a high relief of solid gold. On the king's forehead they had placed a small wreath of flowers, now long withered, that shook Carter's emotions more than the gold that surrounded him.

The second coffin is different from the first, it was found to be decorated using the honeycomb technique in which golden strips are layed down, forming cells that are then filled with a piece of colored glass or semiprecious stones reminiscent of scales or colored feathers. The portrait of the pharaoh is of solid gold. The fact that the features of the king are very different from the two other coffins has suggested to some researchers that originally it could have been made for another recipient.

In the coffin some damage caused by moisture was observed, something that puzzled archaeologists a bit, who could not locate its source. To work better on the coffin it was extracted from the sarcophagus. Excavators were surprised by its enormous weight, and the operation of opening the lid was repeated by pulleys. They opened it and found a third coffin. When removing garlands of flowers and the linen that covered it, they discovered one of the masterpieces of jewelry of all time. The coffin of 1.86 meters in length was made entirely of solid gold, formed by a sheet that was between 2.3 and 2.5 mm thick and weighed 110.4 kg. Now they could explain the exaggerated weight of the set.

Second coffin. The famous solid gold coffin containing the king's mummy was located inside. Some researchers have drawn attention to the fact that the sculpted face on its lid is very different from the other two, which could mean that the coffin would have been made for another recipient.

On top of the gold coffin a generous amount of a black substance had been poured that had filled much of the gap left between the two coffins. The moisture from these ointments was responsible for the damages that were observed in the second sarcophagus. As discussed below, this substance of a plastic-like consistency gave a headache to Carter's team over the course of their research.

Finally, after many years of work and research, Carter, Carnarvon and the world were about to discover the ultimate secret of the Valley of the Kings, the face of the Pharaoh Child.

Transfer of boxes containing the treasures of the tomb. Rail wagons were used, but as there were not enough to cover all the way to the Nile, they would be dismantled as they advanced to reposition them ahead.

Growing Pains

A success as big as this can sometimes hide the many flaws of its protagonists, and this is what happened in part with Howard Carter. To his undeniable tenacity and working capacity should be added the fact that one cannot say he was the friendliest person on earth. Those who met him agree that he was a man who complained of everyone and everything and, as we saw with the incident with French tourists in the Serapeum, diplomacy was not his forte. He had no known friends or any romantic relationships, which has led to more than one researcher to speculate about his possible homosexuality.

But we see here the saying that opposites attract, since there is no news of major problems between Carter and Lord Carnarvon even though the latter was the complete opposite; jovial, friendly, liked to be surrounded with people and everyone liked him.

And although among the two protagonists there seemed to be

considerable harmony, success soon brought them some problems. The first arose after Lord Carnarvon signed an exclusive contract with the Times of London. The agreement was primarily aimed at simplifying relations with the press having a single interlocutor, and through a paper as prestigious as the London newspaper. But nobody eluded that a profitable economic agreement also took place.

This contract was leaving out of the game all other media, since these had to obtain information from the Times, and it felt especially bad in Egypt, where it wasn't understood why they had to know from an English newspaper what happened in Egypt, in a tomb belonging to an ancient Egyptian king.

This was cleverly exploited by local nationalist circles, who considered the situation with King Tut's tomb a clear example of British imperialism.

This political situation would become a major headache for the Carter/Carnarvon team. Egypt had become an independent state a few months before the discovery of the tomb, and many of the new rulers considered foreigners to have too much power and prerogatives, so friction with the authorities was frequent.

To make matters worse Carnarvon died on April 5th, 1923. His widow inherited the concession and continued supporting the work, but from England, with which Carter had to endure alone all the media and political pressure, and as we saw, diplomacy wasn't his forte.

In Carter's book, we see how he repeatedly emphasizes the fact that the tomb had been violated more than once and that many objects had been stolen by thieves in antiquity. His insistence had a very clear reason, and this had nothing to do with archaeology.

In the contract Carnarvon signed with the Egyptian administration when receiving the excavation concession, it was agreed that the distribution of artifacts would be done in equal parts between Egypt and Carnarvon, except in the case that an intact tomb was found, then the content would pass to be owned by Egypt to prevent the assembly was divided and dispersed.

The problem was to clarify what was meant by "intact," hence Carter's insistence in saying that the grave had already been violated at least twice and partly sacked.

For their part, the new Egyptian authorities maintained that a sealed tomb full of treasures was to be regarded as intact and, therefore, all that was within belonged to them.

Tension continued to rise, until one day it exploded. Among other things, the Egyptians came complaining that Carter only allowed his friends into the tomb, while strongly rejecting other people, including some Egyptian authorities. The archaeologist defended himself by the fact that those friends they were referring to were scientists. One day Carter saw how the authorities refused permission to visit the tomb to the wives of several archaeologists invited by him. Carter closed the tomb and paralyzed the excavation in a kind of strike, and the Egyptian authorities replied with the revocation of the concession granted at the time to Lord Carnarvon and the takeover of the work. The case made it to court.

With Carter moved aside, the Egyptian government sought somebody to take over the work, but without any success. Egyptian archaeologists at the time were not capable of assuming such responsibility, and the offer made to the Metropolitan Museum in New

York was politely rejected.

Surely as a form of revenge, the Egyptian authorities allowed hundreds of people a day to visit the grave, knowing the risks that this entailed for both the decorations and for the objects that still remained in the grave.

On March 29th, 1924, while Carter was away from excavations, something happened that was about to multiply problems for him. That day various authorities, accompanied by Egyptian and Western assistants, set out to make an inventory of the parts removed from the tomb so far. They went to the KV-15 tomb, which as we saw earlier was being used as a restoration workshop and warehouse of the recovered objects. The commission was pleasantly surprised by the thoroughness of Carter's work, which included among other things: cataloging each object with a unique reference that was recorded in a triplicate system: in an overall inventory, in the box containing the piece, and then the piece itself.

When they were exiting they noticed that at the bottom of this tomb there were a lot of wooden boxes, most had contained champagne and were now empty, but there was one box that caught the attention of the visitors. It was locked and identified by a label as red wine. They opened it and found something that left them speechless: it was one of the most delicate works of art found in the tomb: a wooden sculpture representing the Pharaoh Child emerging from a lotus flower, made in the unmistakable Amarna style.

What was such a fantastic piece, which didn't appear in any record, doing inside a half-hidden box and with no name tag? Egyptian expedition members were sure from the beginning that Carter was trying to smuggle the item, and so they informed the country's prime minister.

The boy king being born of a lotus flower. This piece was located by the Egyptian authorities hidden in a box with no label and didn't appear on the records of the contents of the tomb. Was Carter trying to keep it illegally?

The hasty explanation given by Carter was that the sculpture had been located under the rubble in the descending corridor between the two boarded up doors that closed the tomb. As it wasn't physically within the chambers of the tomb along with the other pieces, it had not yet been cataloged.

For more than a year the tomb had been opened, and at that time Carter had already published his first volume devoted to the tomb, and he stated that in that hallway were found pieces of objects, but nowhere did he mention this piece despite being one of the most remarkable of those located so far.

Incredibly, the explanation was taken as valid. But perhaps the reason had much to do with the fact that the Director of the Egyptian Antiquities Service, Pierre Lacau, was a staunch advocate of Carter, and that Egyptian authorities didn't find anyone else willing or able to take over works at the tomb.

The truth is that the suspicions that Carter and Lord Carnarvon took small pieces from the tomb without reflecting them in the records were a constant from the very moment of the discovery, and it is also true that in various American and European museums, objects are exhibited under the name of Tut. It is known, for example, that upon Carter's death a number of objects from the tomb, and not on inventories, were reinstated discreetly to the museum of Cairo, and in 2011 the Metropolitan Museum in New York signed an agreement with the Egyptian government for which it returned nineteen pieces that had been removed irregularly from the tomb of Tutankhamun and from the country. Mostly fragments of not a great value, but there were also notable objects such as a small bronze dog.

In 1925 a new pro-Western government came to power in Egypt supported by Britain, and Carter could return to the grave, but only after signing a new contract in which he explicitly renounced the rights to any of the objects located. In return, Lady Almina got 25,000 pounds as compensation for the costs invested so far in the excavation, thus they also protected themselves against possible future claims.

This money was not the only thing that the widow of Lord Carnarvon received at the expense of Egyptian antiquities, since at the death of her husband, she found she had a magnificent private collection of more than 1,200 artifacts from the country of the Nile. Carnarvon had included in his will instructions for the collection to be offered first to the British state for 20,000 pounds, well below the actual value, which was not to the liking of Lady Almina. As she couldn't break the last will of her husband, she gave a clearly insufficient deadline to the British Museum to pay that amount. They, as expected, couldn't raise the money in time.

A. Mace and A. Lucas working on restoration on the box of a chariot, at the door of the tomb KV-15, which served as a warehouse and restoration workshop.

Fulfilled in this way her husband's instructions, she was freed to negotiate the sale with the Metropolitan Museum in New York, who paid the not so modest figure of $145,000 dollars as the British Museum watched helplessly.

In 1928 the tomb was empty, and the work ended there, but Carter's team still needed four more years until all the pieces were properly cataloged and restored.

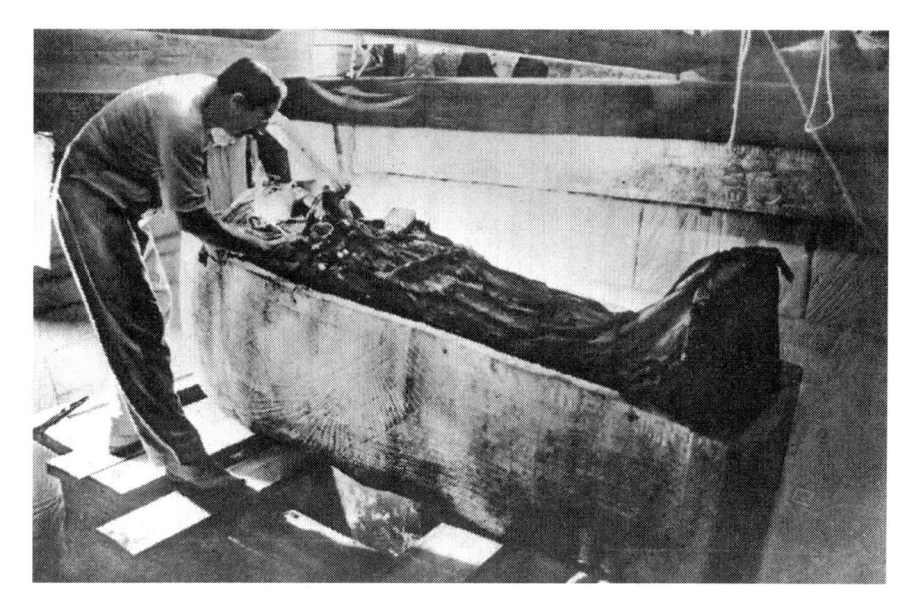

Carter working in a methodical and delicate way in the caskets of Tut. Unfortunately all this patience disappeared when he arrived at the pharaoh's body.

The First Mummy Study, the Carnage.

The first examination of the body of the deceased king was conducted by Dr. Douglas Derry and Saleh Bey Hamdi in 1925, helped by Howard Carter himself; and the effects on the mummy were disastrous. Although in reality the problems for it had begun much earlier.

As we saw earlier, the body had been introduced in three coffins, one inside the other as if they were nesting dolls. The last of them was the famous gold coffin.

Recall that between the last wooden coffin and the gold one, a lot of ointments had been poured, reaching almost to the top. This substance had been poured in a liquid form, but over the centuries it had become a dry blackish mass of plastic consistency and very difficult to remove. This became a serious setback, as it made it very difficult to separate the two coffins.

When they finally were able to open the gold sarcophagus and see the mummy, head and shoulders covered by the well-known gold mask, they encountered again the same problem. The priests had also poured the ointment on the mummy so that it had soaked everything, penetrating between the body and the mask and, upon solidification, had united firmly the mummy with the bottom of the coffin. Unsuccessful attempts were made to separate them.

After the analysis, they concluded that the only way to soften the ointment was the application of heat, and they couldn't think of anything better than to take the coffin outside, with the mummy inside, and leave them exposed to relentless Egyptian midday sun for several hours, in which they got it to reach 65 degrees Celsius. But the plan didn't work and both coffins remained firmly stuck together, with the mummy stuck as well. As discussed below, this operation could have catastrophic results on the body of the pharaoh.

It became clear that the study of the mummy had to take place inside the coffin.

At 9:45 on November 11th, 1925 Douglas Derry, professor of anatomy at the University of Cairo, began the investigation of the Pharaoh Child, helped by Dr. Saleh Bey Hamdi. Also various Egyptian authorities who wanted to witness the historic moment were present.

Ornaments and visible amulets were removed, preserving the golden mask, which as mentioned above was firmly attached to both the mummy and the bottom of the coffin. They began to remove the bandages, which crumbled by touching them. Immediately they realized that the mummy had suffered what seemed some kind of slow internal combustion that had carbonized a good percentage of the body and, of course, the bandages, so that the body was in a regrettable state. The penis had been bandaged in ithyphallic position (erect), holding it at an angle of 90 degrees to the body, and had been preserved reasonably well. To hold it in that position during bandaging, embalmers had introduced a thick straw into the urethra.

Iron knife found among bandages of Tut's mummy. It is one of the first iron objects located in Egypt, along with a charm and a box with miniature tools also found in the tomb. A 2016 study has found that iron used to forge the dagger blade came from a meteorite.

Among the bandages they found a lot of jewelry and amulets, the fingers of both hands and feet were covered with gold caps, and the feet wore sandals of gold. The final tally showed a total of 143 objects scattered throughout the mummy, with their main function to magically protect the body of the pharaoh on his journey to the afterlife. Interestingly, among the many objects of gold and precious stones, one of the pieces that caught the attention of researchers was a simple iron amulet located under the king's head and that, together with a dagger also located on the mummy, which had the blade of this same metal, are two of the oldest iron objects found in Egypt.

I continue to narrate, unable to suppress a sense of astonishment, not without a certain indignation, the process followed by Derry's team to remove the pharaoh from his coffin and retrieving the jewels adorning his body. Unfortunately, it would seem that all the exemplary thoroughness and infinite patience that Carter had shown in the process of studying the tomb and objects contained therein, turned into rush and total lack of consideration when dealing with the king's body.

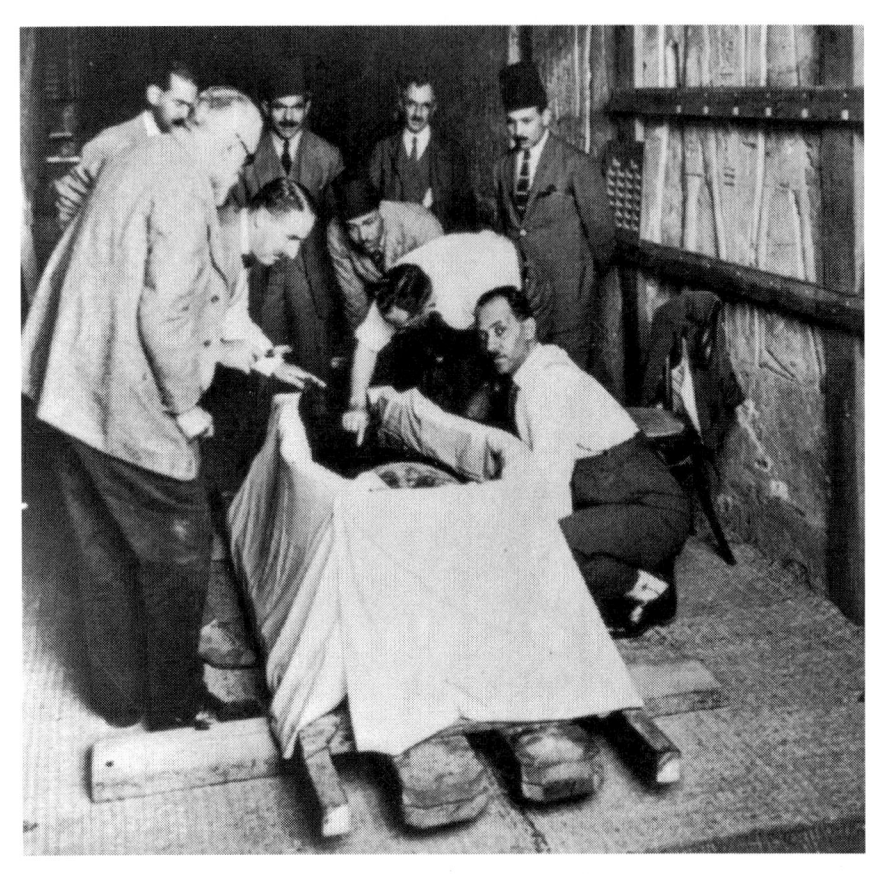

Carter, Derry and the rest of the team during the first autopsy on the body of the pharaoh, who still retains over his head the golden mask.

After they had removed the bandages from the front of the mummy, they were unable to reach the back without removing the body from the coffin. As he was firmly stuck to the bottom, they didn't think twice and Derry, after tearing his legs apart, cut the King's trunk just above the hip. After removing the severed part, they were able to introduce hot knives under the upper trunk until managing to separate it from the coffin, yet the backbone split and the head was left inside the mask, to which, as we mentioned earlier, was solidly attached. Finally they were able to retrieve it using the same system of hot knives. Throughout the process when Derry hit a difficult point, he helped himself to the always effective system of hammer and chisel.

By these methods Carter and Derry managed to separate the mummy from the coffin and mask, but if today another archaeologist dared to repeat these forms of work, most likely he would end up in court.

The end result of all this maneuvering on the mummy was catastrophic. Tutankhamun had been beheaded, his torso split in two and arms and legs separated from the trunk. The king's body was reduced to eighteen disconnected fragments. The mummy had to wait until next year to be rebuilt on a box of sand and returned to his tomb in the first of the wooden coffins.

It is remarkable that at all times Carter remained silent about damage to the mummy, and when they reassembled the dismembered mummy, they joined the separate parts with adhesives, trying to hide the traces of their action. For example, his crossed arms hid the cut that sectioned the body.

We must note here that some researchers say that the sorry state of the mummy after removing the bandages was not due to the action of ointments poured on the body, but mainly due to the fact of exposing it to high temperatures during sun exposure over several hours when they tried to melt the ointment. This likely produced a rapid carbonization of the tissue, leading to cracks. Let us also remember here that Carter himself describes the color of the mummy at the time of removing the bandages as whitish/gray, while the image of Tutankhamun we all have in mind is that of a black as coal body, which makes evident that there was a rapid deterioration of tissues after exposure to air.

After removing the mummy, the gold and wooden coffins remained firmly united by ointments. To separate them the gold coffin was internally covered with thick zinc plates, it was flipped over and were placed underneath several paraffin lamps at full power until they reached a temperature of 500 degrees. The temperature was maintained for several hours until it was possible to melt the ointments and separate the two coffins.

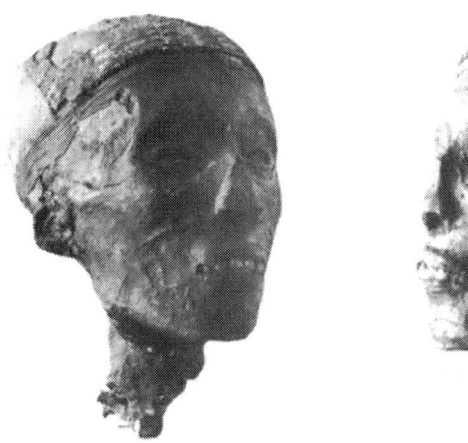

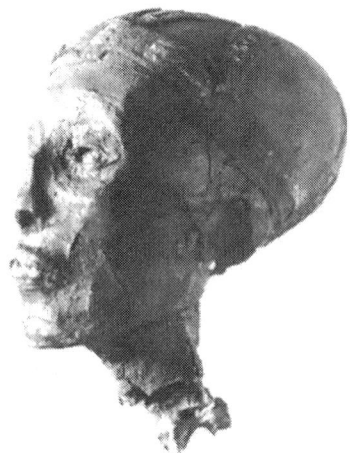

Head of Tutankhamun's mummy separate from the trunk during the autopsy.

The Child Pharaoh's mummy recomposed on a bed of sand once Dr. Derry's study was completed. Today the mummy shows damage that would have occurred at some unspecified time after taking this picture.

What was the Cause of Death of the "Pharaoh Child"?

This is one of the questions that has been repeated over and over since there was record of the existence of this pharaoh, of the fact that he reigned for only nine or ten years and that he died so young. To unravel this mystery there's been several studies—some more aggressive than others—conducted on the mummy since it was discovered.

We've already talked about the first test, which despite much destruction, obtained poor results. Derry could only discover that Tutankhamun measured approximately 1.67 meters, died at approximately 17 to 19 years of age (most likely at 18); his skull bore a great similarity with the mummy located in the tomb KV-55, which was believed to be Akhenaten, with which a close relationship was probable; and that the golden mask reflected quite accurately the characteristics of the deceased, a point of considerable importance to art history.

In 1968, the Tutankhamun's mummy was again taken from its grave to be subjected to an X-ray study, which was conducted by a team from the University of Liverpool (UK) led by Dr. R.G. Harrison. Using portable equipment, about 50 plates were taken of the entire body.

This study confirmed several of the proposals made by Derry after the first autopsy. The age of death would be about 18, and the skull had very similar measures to that of Akhenaten, but added important details such as the missing breastbone, part of the right clavicle, and ribs on the front of the body. Extremes such that, surprisingly, were overlooked by Derry and Carter. Harrison also caused a great deal of confusion when indicating that the king's skull presented inside a piece of loose bone and an area on its wall that was too thin, which could have been caused by internal bleeding, in turn caused by a blow. In addition researchers found that the king's penis had disappeared.

The media immediately echoed the news of the discovery of possible head injuries, speaking directly of murder as a possible cause of death of the Boy Pharaoh.

And here's where we find another mystery because, as we mentioned, at present the mummy lacks the sternum and ribs, which seem cut off, and part of the right clavicle is missing. But if we look closely at the pictures that Harry Burton performed after the 1925 autopsy, we can perfectly distinguish both clavicles and ribs seem visible under the necklaces that adorned the mummy.

According to this, the disappearance of these bones had occurred during manipulations between the completion of the autopsy and the realization of x-rays in 1968. Let's not forget that the body was returned to the tomb with some gold jewelry attached to the chest plus a tiara on the forehead. Those jewels are missing now, so it is conceivable to think that in this intervening time someone damaged the body when snatching the jewelry.

But the documented damage in the chest of the mummy has also led some researchers to propose various causes for the king's death, some more or less picturesque. Dr. R. W. Harer proposed in 2006 that the king might have died from a hippopotamus attack, as he would have been bitten in the chest, breaking it apart with its very powerful jaws. The same author later changed his mind and in 2011 proposed as a possible cause of death a horse's kick, which would have broken his chest.

A new study of the 1968 radiographs performed in 2001, revealed that there had been errors in its interpretation, since there were no anomalies in the walls of the skull and the two bone fragments that appear loose inside the cranial vault seem to have come from the first cervical vertebra. These would have been released and penetrated the skull during the inspection of the mummy by Derry in 1925, as he introduced a metal rod through a hole in the nape to see inside the skull. The 2001 study also confirmed the presence of solidified resin inside the skull, which had been introduced by the nostrils in liquid state after removal of the brain.

In 1978, the dentist J. Harris took a series of high-resolution X-rays to study the pharaoh's teeth. The study would also include a blood test. The most remarkable result is that this author believes that Tutankhamun died at a more advanced age, specifically 21-22 years, a result that is not shared by most researchers.

A fourth study was conducted in 2005, and for this the most advanced medical technology available was used: computed tomography.

A mobile scanner mounted on a truck was taken to the entrance of the tomb and for fifteen minutes, the bowels of our mummy were digitally crumbled to show us— after 1,700 radiographs—images never seen before, and more importantly, to provide scientists crucial information to know the life and death of the most famous pharaoh in history.

As expected the data has clarified many of the questions of investigators. On the one hand they confirmed the results of the second study of radiographs. There are no signs of fractures or blows to the skull, so the theories about conspiracies and assassinations that circulated, and that had even given a name to the alleged murderers, were thrown to the ground.

The small hole in the nape of which we spoke earlier was probably performed by Dr. Derry, and through which most likely penetrated the bone fragments found in 1968 inside the skull.

But while eliminating a possible cause of the death of the king, another one was found. Scientists located a possible fracture in his left leg produced shortly before his death, since it hadn't healed completely. This makes us suspect a supervening infection as a result of the fracture likely causing the death.

But the study did not stop there, as it provided other important data such as the realization that Tutankhamun had a malformation in his left foot, specifically a vascular bone necrosis. A condition that prevents blood from the bones to circulate properly. This illness caused his foot to twist inwards, which would prevent him from supporting himself fully, and therefore would cause a pronounced limp. This would explain the striking presence of some 130 canes in the tomb, which had led some authors to speculate that the king collected them. Now we know it was not a hobby but a necessity.

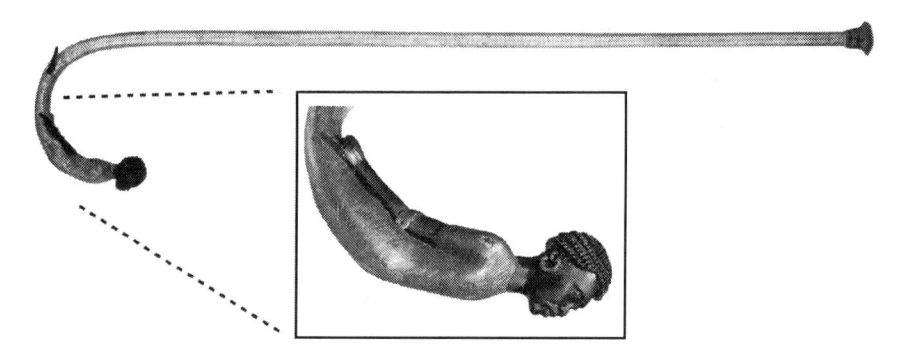

One of the many canes located inside the tomb. It shows a "Nubian" in the handle.

The study also revealed that Tutankhamun had his heart removed during the embalming process, something very rare in the mummies of the time. Nor had any scarab been placed inside his chest, which was also quite common.

Finally, this study also served to locate Tutankhamun's penis, which as we mentioned was noted to be missing during the radiographic study of 1968. Despite the many theories which had flourished at that time to explain the disappearance of the royal pecker, even suggesting plots and conspiracies of the darkest interests, the reality could not be simpler. With so much hustle and bustle, the pharaoh's penis had detached from the body and had been buried in the sand on which the king rested. A little bit of glue and Tut presents again his royal manhood intact for the rest of eternity.

2010 has seen the light of the latest study on Tutankhamun, a DNA analysis affecting not only the pharaoh, but ten other mummies related to Tut. This analysis has been of paramount importance, as it has allowed to clarify once and for all the identity of Tut's parents. On the one hand, it is confirmed that his father is the mummy located in the KV-55 tomb whom had always been identified as Akhenaten, while his mother would be the known as "young lady," an unidentified mummy located in 1898 by Victor Loret in the tomb KV-35. Analyses have revealed that this woman would also be a sister of Akhenaten.

Another important conclusion reached in this study is that King Tut suffered from birth a series of physical problems caused largely by inbreeding in his family. Evidence of the presence of tropical malaria, the most dangerous form of the disease, were also discovered.

The poor health of the monarch might have been the reason that he didn't overcome a possible complication of the leg fracture.

Keep in mind that not all researchers agree with the way they have done both the sample collection and DNA testing, so we can't guarantee 100% everything that has been said about the causes and circumstances surrounding the death of the boy king.

As we can see, we have moved from the first hypothesis of the death of the young king as an assassination in a palace conspiracy, to being attacked by a hippo, to kicked by a horse, to finally the sad existence of a sickly, crippled child, weakened by the continuous incest of his ancestors, who could not overcome the infection caused by a broken leg. A lot less epic, but perhaps more humane end for a unique young man who has turned into an evergreen icon of ancient Egypt.

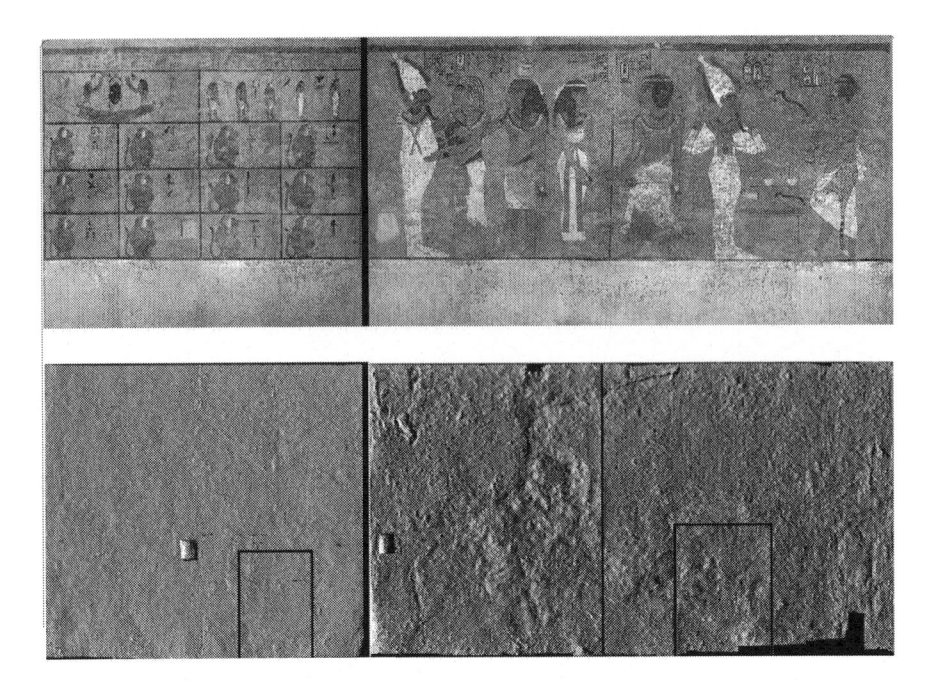

At the top, photographs of the west (left) and north (right) walls of the Tutankhamun's burial chamber. Below, images of the same walls scanned by Factum Arte. In both the positions of the alleged secret chambers entries are displayed, according to Reeves. On the north wall, the vertical line indicates the width of the original hall, which is supposed to continue behind the wall.

Is Nefertiti in KV-62?

On April 30, 2014 was inaugurated at the entrance of the Valley of the Kings an exact replica of Tutankhamun's tomb, built in Madrid by the company Factum Arte. This work was commissioned by the Egyptian government, concerned about the preservation of the original tomb. To achieve a perfect result, every detail of the tomb of the Pharaoh Child was photographed and scanned in high resolution. The images resulting from these detailed works were uploaded to the website of Factum Arte so they could be consulted online.

In June 2015, the prestigious British Egyptologist Nicholas Reeves published an article that launched the world a surprising theory. He thought he knew where the tomb of Queen Nefertiti was, nothing less than inside the most famous tomb of Egypt: the one of Tutankhamun. Not only that, but he thought that inside that tomb would be a second secret chamber hitherto unknown.

To reach that conclusion he studied carefully the images obtained by Factum Arte. He thought he had found cracks and fissures that indicate the existence of a hidden door in the west wall of the burial chamber, while in the north wall there would be signs that the chamber originally continued in that direction.

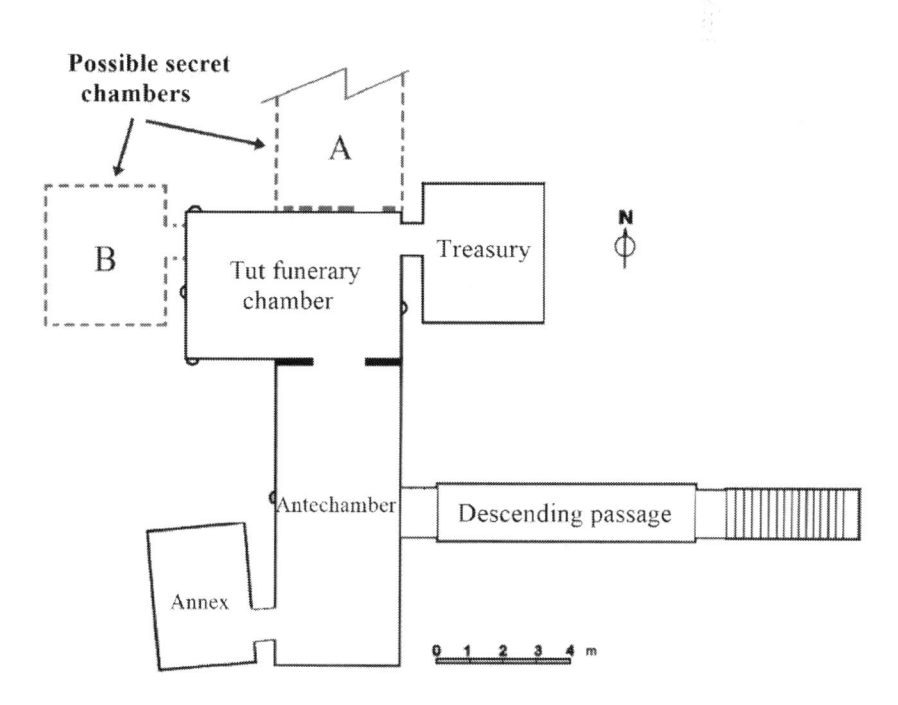

Plan of Tutankhamun's tomb with possible secret chambers. According Reeves, chamber A would actually be the continuation of the original antechamber, so it has its same width. Nefertiti's tomb would be there. Chamber B would have been built in the time of King Tut, then, it would be contemporary to the burial chamber. Drawing of the author.

According to the theory of Reeves, the KV-62 tomb would not have been originally built for King Tut, hypotheses already expressed by other researchers since it was discovered in 1922. But the novelty is that the British researcher indicates that the owner of this tomb is still in the grave, but to accommodate the newcomer, what was done was to divide the original tomb by a wall and extended the existing corridor to build the burial chamber where Tutankhamun was found. Thus, what we now know as antechamber of the tomb, originally would be a long, wide corridor at least twice the length of the current, and at the end of this could be Nefertiti chamber.

To verify the Reeves theory, extensive studies are being developed inside the tomb using the latest available technologies: infrared and ground penetrating radar, which can help us to know what is behind the walls without touching them.

So far the results look promising, because in March 2016 the Egyptian minister of antiquities indicated that the study of GPR conducted by a Japanese team seemed to confirm, with 90 percent certainty, the existence of the two hidden chambers indicated by Reeves, and not only that, but also seemed to indicate the existence of metal and organic material behind one of the walls.

But there are many scientists who disagree with Reeves, including the once all-powerful minister of antiquities Zahi Hawass, who has declared that: "The Reeves theory has no scientific basis", or that all this: "Is an absurdity ".

The latest statements by the Egyptian authorities seem to be more cautious. And today it is difficult to distinguish the scientific true from the maneuverings to attract tourism, an activity that today is in the doldrums in the country of the Nile. It seems that we'll still have to wait some time to see if the tomb of King Tutankhamun still keeps more "wonderful things".

Lord Carnarvon and his wife during a horse race in 192. At that time he was not aware that two years later, his death will unleash an unstoppable psychosis.

Second Part: the Curse of the Mummies

The Beginning of Madness

On February 28th, 1923, a few days after the solemn opening of Tutankhamun's burial chamber, Lord Carnarvon went to Aswan for some rest. There he was bitten by a mosquito on his left cheek and a few days later, when shaving, he cut himself in the swollen area (in 1925 when the first inspection of the mummy of Tutankhamun took place, they discovered that the king had a scar on his left cheek, about the same place where Carnarvon cut himself).

Carnarvon soon began to feel tired and with a small fever, so he laid up on the advice of his daughter Evelyn, who had accompanied him there. For a few days he appeared to improve, with which he was able to get up from bed, but a few hours later his condition worsened and he had to lie down again.

His daughter became concerned and moved him to Cairo. As his condition worsened she urgently telegraphed her mother, who traveled from England by plane immediately along with her father's personal physician, Dr. Johnson. As soon as Carter was told by Lady Evelyn of the news, he also traveled to the Continental Hotel, arriving around the same time as Carnarvon's son, Porchey, who had come from India. Carter discovered his patron dying.

At ten minutes to two in the morning of April 5, 1923 Lord Carnarvon died at 57 years old. His last words were: "I have heard his call and I follow it". According to his son, at the moment of his father's death there was a blackout in Cairo forcing everyone to bring candles to his room.

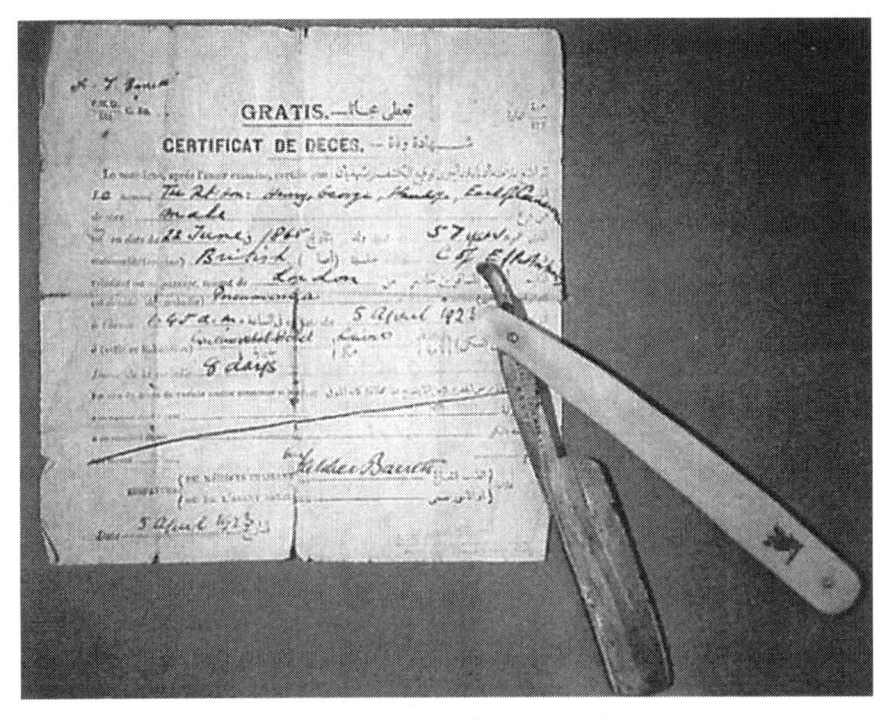

Lord Carnarvon's death certificate and knife with which he cut himself shaving. The infection led him to the grave.

In his medical certificate the cause of death is listed as pneumonia, which would have been caused by complications from the infection of the bite.

Upon arriving with Lord Carnarvon's corpse at his Highclere

estate in England, his dog Susie, who had accompanied him many times on their trips to Egypt, began to howl and died suddenly (other accounts say that the death of the dog was simultaneous to that of Carnarvon's).

This was the origin of the so-called "curse of Tutankhamun" that inexplicably spread like wildfire, amplified at every step and appearing in the media around the world.

We must remember that even before the discovery of the famous tomb, stories about curses of mummies and tombs were very popular and had even been captured in books and taken to the stage.

In 1827, the English playwright Jane C. Loudon Webb had premiered the play "The Mummy". In 1845, Edgar Allan Poe published the story "Conversations With a Mummy" while the creator of "Little Women," Louisa May Alcott, published in 1869 "Lost in the Pyramid: The Curse of the Mummy". In 1903, Bram Stoker published "The Jewel of the Seven Stars," which would be adapted to the creation of the famous film "The Mummy," released in 1932 with Boris Karloff as the main protagonist.

But undoubtedly the most famous story about cursed mummies born before the discovery of Tutankhamun's tomb was Titanic's mummy.

According to the most widespread version of this legend (like all those we will discuss it has multiple versions), the most famous sinking in history was caused by the fact that the ship was also carrying on board the mummy of an Egyptian priestess that a rich American had bought to the British Museum. Given its high value, the mummy hadn't been stored in the holds with other luggage, but in a cabin located just behind the bridge of the ship. From the time of its purchase in Egypt, this mummy would have caused numerous deaths and misfortunes to its successive owners, who came to say that an evil spirit was living in its eyes, which was the reason why it was finally donated to the British Museum. After many protests by museum guards who complained of screams and strange noises coming from the coffin, and the death of one of the guards, which was also blamed on the mummy, it would have been first removed from the showcase and then moved to the basement of the museum and eventually sold.

The one known as "Unlucky mummy". Actually the lid of an interior coffin which is preserved in the British Museum in London.

Of course, in the records of the cargo being carried by the Titanic, no mummy shows up, nor is there evidence of any survivor commenting about sharing the lifeboat with such companion, of which that person would surely remember. And according to legend, the mummy was saved from the sinking and continued causing calamities, each more absurd.

What those stories often forget is that in reality such a mummy doesn't exist. The so-called "Unlucky Mummy," is actually no more than the lid of an interior coffin which is preserved in the British Museum, and this piece could hardly have caused the misfortunes attributed to it by half the world, especially the collapse of the Titanic. It started to be part of their funds in 1889, donated by Arthur F. Wheeler, who was the man who brought it from Egypt. It has since then only abandoned its showcases on two occasions, once in 1990 to join an exhibition in Australia, and another for the same reason in 2007, this time bound for Taiwan.

Newspaper clippings from different countries of the world. The news related to the curse spreads.

Psychosis Spreads

Lord Carnarvon had just died and the press started talking about the tomb being cursed. Let's recall that when the discovery took place, Carnarvon had an exclusive deal to report all related findings to the Times of London, so reporters roamed the Valley of the Kings hunting for any news that might enrich the official information from the British newspaper, identical for all media. Of course, the more sensational the news was, the better.

One of the main broadcasters of this psychosis was the famous British writer Marie Corelli, who wrote an article in British and American newspapers in which he included the following comment:

> "I can't stop thinking about the risks to disturb the repose of a king of Egypt, whose tomb is special and solemnly kept, and steal some of his possessions. According to a book that I have entitled 'The Ancient History of the Pyramids' (an ancient Arabic text), '... the most terrible punishment will befall the reckless who profane a sealed tomb.' So I wonder, was a mosquito bite really what severely infected Lord Carnarvon?".

Corelli's article was "retouched" by other journalists, who said that the curse was written on a wall of the tomb, while others told another version, according to which the curse was not on the wall but in an ostrakon (a stone or ceramic plate used to take notes). According to the story, at first the ostrakon was ignored, but when Alan Gardiner deciphered it, it turned out it contained the following curse: "death will strike with its pitchfork that who disturbs the Pharaoh's sleep".

Whatever the chosen version of the story, it's said the text had been hidden away by Carter and erased from inventories to not frighten the superstitious workers.

To these invented facts others were added, quite possibly just as false. According to one, Carter would have been stung by a scorpion just the day before the discovery of the tomb. It is assumed that the gods warned him not to be further digging in such a place.

Also very famous was the mysterious case of the Carter's canary. Apparently, the archaeologist had in his house a cage with a bird that kept him company. One day he heard it chirping and fluttering, and then all was quiet. When Carter looked he saw horrified that a cobra had just devoured the bird. Let's not forget that the cobra was the representation of Wadjet, patron goddess of the pharaohs.

And everyone was aware of any fact or detail that could be attributed to the supposed curse. One day, for example, a hawk was seen flying over the Valley of the Kings that then got lost in the west, a cardinal point where according to the ancient Egyptians the afterlife was located. Those present took it as a sign from God. "These people will find gold and death," they commented.

Six months after Lord Carnarvon's death, his little brother, the political and diplomatic Aubrey Herbert, died in a peculiar way. Aubrey had endured vision problems for much of his life, but shortly before his death in September 1923 he went completely blind. We don't know how a person of his statute would listen to a charlatan who convinced him that if he tore out all of his teeth he would regain his vision, but that's exactly what he did. The extraction was carried out but resulted in a blood infection, septicemia, which led him to the grave.

Shortly afterward the nun who had attended Carnarvon's bedside also suddenly died.

The deaths continued, and for journalists all were inexplicable. In 1923, shortly after the death of Lord Carnarvon, his friend the American railroad magnate George Jay Gould, traveled to Egypt and didn't miss the opportunity to visit Tut's tomb, who Carter himself showed to him. The next morning he awoke with high fever. He seemed to recover, but died shortly after in the French Riviera. Doctors at first didn't know what to attribute his death to, but later indicated that it could be nothing less than the bubonic plague.

Of the deaths attributed to the curse, we highlight that of

Carter's secretary, Richard Bethell, in 1929, as it was the beginning of a string of misfortunes that newspapers never tired of airing.

Bethell was found dead in her bed and the doctors diagnosed as a cause of death circulatory collapse. When his father heard the news he committed suicide by jumping from the window of his London home, located on the seventh floor. To complete the misfortune, when her body was taken to the cemetery, the hearse ran over an eight year old child killing him.

The existence of curses on tombs (royal or not), sculptures and other more or less sacred objects, is not uncommon in Egypt or in other ancient cultures, as in the Roman world, where the so called *tabulae defixionis* are common. These are texts usually written on sheets of lead that were placed in tombs, temples or wells with magic formulas wishing misfortunes on certain people.

In Egypt many inscriptions with curses have been located, and they predict very different punishments on those who disturb the repose of the dead, damage the grave or steal the statues or offerings from funeral chapels. Among the punishments with which they threaten, we can highlight the following:

— Will be wretched and persecuted (Penuiut's Tomb, XX Dynasty)

— His name will no longer exist in the land of Egypt (Statue of high priest Heritor, XX-XXI Dynasty.)

— I will strangle his neck like a goose (Inscription from Hermeru of the VI Dynasty)

— A donkey will rape him and a donkey will rape his wife (Graphite No. 11 from Deir el Bahari XX Dynasty.)

But verifying the falsity of many of the alleged consequences of the curse is not difficult. Even today it's possible to find online information that not only exaggerate the number of dead, but come to blatantly distort the dates of death of many of them, when the truth is that, according to the study by Herbert E. Winlock, director of the Metropolitan Museum in New York, of the 26 people present at the opening of the tomb, only six died within the next ten years. Of the 22 present at the opening of the sarcophagus, only two died in the next ten years; and of the ten present at the autopsy in 1925, none died within ten years. Also, if the ages of the deceased are observed, it can be seen that in most cases, these are within the life expectancies for the early twentieth century in Egypt, and in some cases much higher, as in the case of Lady Almina, Carnarvon's wife, who despite having been many times in the grave and having continued financing the study of its contents on the death of her husband, died in 1969 in Bristol, at the not inconsiderable age of 92 years, and the cause of her death was none other than a piece of meat stew that got stuck in her windpipe and choked her.

2002 is the date of a study took place by researcher Mark R. Nelson from Monash University in Melbourne to try to scientifically prove the inconsistency of the supposed curse. He analyzed a group of 44 people of Western origin who were in Egypt at the time of the discovery of Tutankhamun's tomb. Of these, 25 were in direct contact to it, either because they participated in the opening of the tomb, of the chapels and coffins or in the study of the mummy.

The results indicate that the average age of death of people who didn't have any contact with these tasks was 75 years of age, while those who were involved in this work died with an average age of 70 years. We see that there is a difference of five years, although this small variation is considered normal when working with such small samples.

But perhaps the main evidence that there has been no curse is found in the two persons who may have had more reason to provoke the wrath of the deceased pharaoh than anyone: Howard Carter and Douglas Derry. The first was the man responsible for the discovery and the person who spent the most time in the grave, and the second was the main culprit of the dismemberment of the king's mummy.

Well, Carter died in 1939, at 65 years of age, while Derry didn't die until 1969, at age 87. Any comment about a curse would be superfluous.

Despite all the evidence showing that no supernatural force had claimed the lives of all those people, superstition is very strong, and many people still blindly believe in the factuality of the curse. Although we must not forget that this also had some positive consequences. For example, during the 20s and 30s of last century, when a situation of almost generalized panic had been reached, there were many who got rid of all Egyptian antiquities they had been collecting following the fashion of those years. Most of these pieces ended up in European and American museums, where we can continue enjoying them today.

And we shouldn't leave aside the benefits that the discovery of Tutankhamun's tomb (with or without cursing) brought to Egypt, as it made tourism soar into the land of the Nile, tourism that despite not being in the best moment, has grown steadily over the decades, leading to millions of people to enjoy not only the treasures of the boy king, but the immense Egyptian cultural heritage.

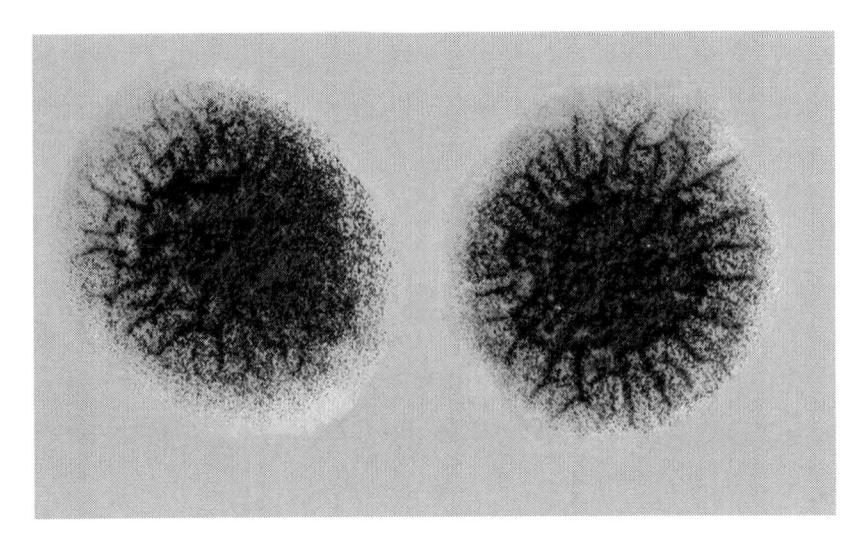

Enlarged image of the fungus Aspergirus Niger, which has been identified as one of the possible responsible for the death of several people who had been in graves or had manipulated mummies, papyri and other objects found within them. Spores of this fungus were found by researchers in numerous employees of Egyptian museums.

Possible Explanations of the Deaths

Although we have seen that the age at death of all these people falls within the normal span among populations born during the second half of the nineteenth century, there have been several more attempts to explain the various deaths related to the alleged curse.

For example, they emphasize the fact that Lord Carnarvon died of pneumonia, which is not at all strange if we remember that he was in Egypt precisely because of his respiratory problems. It falls within the expected lifespan for someone of his background, and when antibiotics were still in experimental phase, an infection could degenerate into pneumonia and take him to the grave.

Regarding the alleged blackout in Cairo at the time of Lord Carnarvon's death, researchers point out that until recently these cuts in electric supply were not uncommon.

Other researchers have chosen to try to identify possible elements that could favor in one way or another an early mortality of the staff that worked directly in the tombs or with mummies, developing various theories:

Poison.- According to this theory, Egyptian priests had been able to develop poisons, based on animals and plants, able to withstand thousands of years in the closed environment of the tomb, so that anyone who entered them died. So far no one has found the slightest trace of these potential poisons.

Fungi.- This theory was launched by Dr. Ezzedine Taha from the University of Cairo, which announced having found traces of the fungus *Aspergillus niger* in many museum employees who had worked with mummies and other artifacts from Egyptian tombs. This fungi usually does not cause death, but respiratory system inflammation and fever, two of the symptoms many of the deceased had. And of course, they had the capacity to aggravate other existing ailments, often resulting in death.

We must remember that Carter himself tells us that on the walls of the burial chamber (not in the other ones) there were fungal groups he blamed on plaster moisture from the walls.

Dr. Taha also indicates that throughout history there had been many researchers that after working continuously with ancient papyrus had suffered respiratory problems and skin irritation, symptoms known as "Coptic itch". According to this researcher the same fungi may also cause other more serious conditions.

Ezzedin Taha released the results of these studies in a press conference on November 3rd, 1962, announcing that he had dismantled the theory of the curse of the mummies. Unfortunately, after the press conference, and when Taha was driving his car along with two other collaborators between Suez and Cairo, the car suddenly veered to the left hitting another oncoming vehicle. Taha and his two companions died on the spot while the occupants of the other vehicle were injured. According to the autopsy Dr. Taha had suffered a circulatory collapse. As you might imagine, proponents of the existence of the curse had a very clear idea about the real reason behind his death.

Years later, Italian doctor Nicola Di Paolo added another fungus to the Dr. Taha's list of suspects: *Aspergillus ochraceus*, while in 1999 German microbiologist Gottahard Krame, from the University of Leipzig, having examined 40 mummies, identified a number of spores from different fungi that had survived thousands of years in good condition. Although most were harmless, there were some potentially dangerous ones.

The danger of fungi was proven in 1973 in another place far from Egypt: the crypt of Wawel Castle in Poland, where King Casimir III rested. That year a group of archaeologists unearthed the remains of the King for a study. A few years later, twelve of the fourteen investigators who handled the remains died.

One of the two survivors proposed to determine the cause of the deaths of his comrades, and found fungi on objects placed in the tomb and even in one of the femurs of the King: *Aspergillus flavus* and *Aspergillus niger*.

Histoplasmosis.- For proponents of this theory, the culprits behind many of the health problems of Egyptologists and even of some deaths would be none other than bats. The feces from these flying rodents thrives the Histoplasma fungus, which produces a disease that manifests as fever and respiratory problems in the system and can be fatal.

Some have pointed out that Tut's tomb was sealed, so it was impossible to have bats inside, but the truth is that, once opened, it was barely closed by means of two railings on the interior and exterior doors, so that the presence of bats sheltering inside the tomb was probable, although we doubt very much that a few of these excretions could cause more health problems than the regular ones on the outside, where there was a lot more dirt.

Radioactivity.-Another theory, that is rather shocking is that which attributed deaths to the absorption of high doses of radioactivity, causing fatigue at the beginning and in many cases circulatory collapse which may lead to death. Proponents of this theory are of the opinion that the Egyptians knew the effects of radioactive materials and placed them in tombs to stop intruders.

The truth is that readings have been taken in many tombs and no more radioactivity was detected than the logical levels of radon gas (which occurs naturally), and always within normal parameters.

As we can see there have been many attempts to find the reason behind deaths that others have attributed to the curse, and the only one that can effectively be related to these deaths is that which refers to the presence of certain fungi, a fact that can be proven scientifically along with their harmful effects. The rest of the theories are merely speculations as unscientific as the curse itself.

View of the entrance to the Pharaoh Tutankhamun exhibition installed at the Field Museum of Natural History in Chicago (Illinois-USA) in 2006. Exhibitions like this, with elements from the tomb of Tut (authentic or reproductions) have traveled the world with great success.

Conclusion

In the preceding pages we have made a quick review of the circumstances surrounding one of the greatest archaeological discoveries of the world and of all time, and we have done so by looking in its spotlight but also in its shadows; in the blinding glare of gold that filled the tomb, while not forgetting the miseries of the men who made this fabulous discovery possible, but were also responsible for the sad end of a humiliated and torn apart king.

Few Egyptian pharaohs suffered after their death so many outrages in their bodies as Tutankhamun did, but according to ancient Egyptian beliefs, a person does not totally die while his name is still spoken by future generations. If so, the Pharaoh Child, despite all the sorrow, will be happy wherever he might be, because if there is a king in Egypt whose name is known and pronounced every day around the world, it would be the name Tutankhamun.

THIRD BOOK

The Silver Pharaohs

Hawk head from the silver casket containing the remains of Pharaoh Sheshonq II, located at the royal necropolis of Tanis.

Introduction

On February 27th, 1939, while Europe looked askance at Germany, and while Hitler continued his political maneuvers and verbal escalations, a French Egyptologist, Pierre Montet, entered into what looked like a tomb plundered many centuries ago among the fertile palm groves of the Nile Delta. On the walls of the underground chamber could be seen engraved the name of Takelot II, sovereign of the XXII Dynasty. What that man had just discovered was nothing less than the lost Necropolis of the Pharaohs of Tanis.

On March 20th of that year, in the same place, Montet had an even more spectacular discovery; while German troops settled into Czechoslovakia after the invasion of Bohemia and Moravia in a trial of what in a few months after would be the conquest of Poland; the Frenchman found the intact tomb of King Sheshonq II. And within a hidden chamber of that same grave, another pharaoh —Psusennes I— still awaited surrounded by immense treasures.

This poor timing between the discovery of the royal tombs of

Tanis and the escalating war in Europe was the main reason why almost no one back then was aware of the important discovery, and the reason why, even today, while visitors to the Egyptian Museum in Cairo crowd the galleries that keep the treasures found in the tomb of Tutankhamun, there are few who spend more than a cursory glance at the nearest keeping room dedicated to the findings in the Tanis necropolis.

View of the Egyptian Museum in Cairo. Upstairs both the treasures of Tutankhamun's tomb as those of the royal tombs of Tanis are displayed.

The boy-pharaoh was fortunate that his tomb was discovered in 1922, during the "Roaring 20s," a period of peace and optimism in which newspapers from half the world were stationed at the tomb of the Valley of the Kings to give a full account of everything surrounding the discovery. By contrast, Sheshonq, Psusennes and their people appeared at a time when the world was preparing for the biggest catastrophe suffered (and caused) by humans since the time of our origin; that would end the lives of 50 million souls. The thoughts and fears of the world at that point were far from Egypt, more centered on those beginning to die in Europe than those whom had died 3,000 years ago on the banks of the Nile.

This is the story of that discovery.

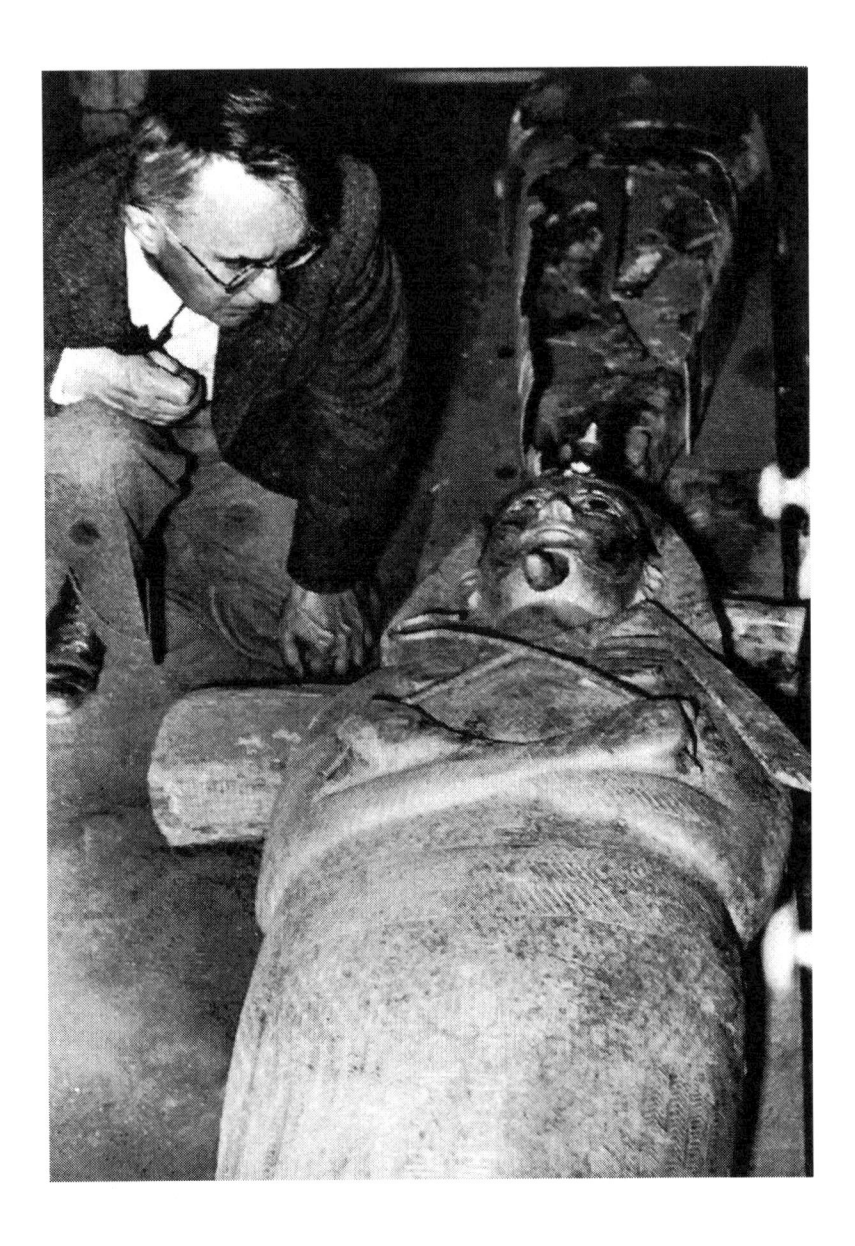

Pierre Montet inspects the silver sarcophagus of Pharaoh Psusennes I shortly after its discovery.

Pierre Montet and Tanis

Often we read that the discovery of the royal tombs of Tanis was a fluke, and this is something I think is really unfair to their discoverer, since no one can say that making a discovery after eleven years of hard work in the same field is accidental. It's true, however, that Montet was not specifically looking for these royal tombs; but the truth is that no archaeologist really knows what is going to find by digging underground, no matter what he's looking for, and that's part of the magic of archaeology.

Pierre Marie Montet was born on June 27th, 1885 in Villefranche sur-Saône, capital of the historical region of Beaujolais, famous for its wines, and his studies soon headed for Egyptology, and in 1910 he achieved his dream of going to the country of the Nile through a scholarship from the French Institute of Oriental Archaeology.

Between 1911 and 1913 he dug in various places like Kasr es-Sayad, Siout, Der Rifeh and the important necropolis of Beni-Hassan. He describes part of his job there in this way:

"I was able to compare texts, draw some scenes and details that had been collected somewhat schematically in M. Newberry's art prints and inaccurately in Champollion and Rosellini's"

Between 1913 and 1914 he excavated the necropolis of Abou Roach, where he discovered several tombs of the first dynasty. But the outbreak of World War I led him to the front, where he appeared in several battles in which he was wounded but also awarded for his service.

Nineteenth century engraving showing the remains found after excavations on the *Tel* of San-el Hagar in 1878.

After the war, he devoted time to teaching at the University of Strasbourg. But the East was calling him, so in 1920 he moved to Byblos in ancient Phoenicia, and for five years directed the excavation of this port city, which in ancient times was a hub of intense trade with

Pharaonic Egypt.

In 1928 the French government commissioned him to dig in San el-Hagar and guaranteed an annual allocation. Finally, in 1929, Egypt signed a concession which allowed Montent to head to the Nile Delta. Beside San el-Hagar raised an imposing *tell*. A tell is a hill formed by overlapping structures built by men over many centuries, and by falling down and getting covered by sand coming from the nearby desert creates an elevation that gradually takes on the appearance of a natural formation. It was there that Montet expected to find evidence of ancient contacts between the Pharaonic and Semitic worlds:

"On the shores of Syria I searched and found traces of the Egyptians. Tanis seemed to me, then, the town of Egypt where there were more chances of finding traces of the Semites ".

This evidence of the contacts had already been found in Byblos, but he also hoped to find evidence of an Egyptian pharaoh's attack on the Jewish capital that appears in the Old Testament:

"In the fifth year of king Rehoboam, Shishak king of Egypt attacked Jerusalem.—because *(its people)* were not faithful to the Lord — with twelve hundred chariots and sixty thousand horsemen; And no one could tell the people that came with him from Egypt: Libyans, Cushites and Ethiopians. He took the fortified cities of Judah and arrived to Jerusalem ...

... Rose, then, Shishak king of Egypt against Jerusalem and he took away the treasures of the house of Yahweh and the treasures of the royal house. He took it all, and also took the golden shields made by Solomon. " (1 Kings 14)

Montet identified that Shishak with Sheshonq I, Pharaoh founder of the XXII Dynasty that had reigned between 945 and 924 BC, so he tried to find in Tanis traces of the invasion of Israel and, why not? Some of the objects looted from the temple of King Solomon. Some researchers go further and say the secret goal of Montet was nothing less than to locate the Ark of the Covenant, which supposedly stored the tablets of the laws that Yahweh had given to Moses. In fact, this information was used by American filmmaker Steven Spielberg to develop the plot of his film *Raiders of the Lost Ark*, in which we can recall were the Nazis who digged in Tanis looking for that sacred object.

Montet didn't find the treasures of King Solomon's temple, but as we know, he found others that were equally or more spectacular than those of the biblical monarch.

In total Montet excavated in Tanis for fifteen annual campaigns between 1929 and 1951, with a break between 1941 and 1944 motivated by the Second World War. In fact the work on this exceptional site has continued to this day through new generations of excavators.

Image of the Pierre Montet excavations at Tanis. Next to the statue of Ramses we can see his own daughter playing.

Tanis

In the northeast of the Nile Delta, next to one of the many branches of the river, we find the city of San el-Hagar, and very close to it, on a sandy hill visible from a great distance, the ruins of what once was the Djanet of ancient Egyptians or the Zoan of the Bible. But like many other places in Egypt it has come to us instead with its Greek name: Tanis; the former capital of the nineteenth *nome* (province) of Lower Egypt during the Third Intermediate Period (c. 1069-664 BC), and that was favored by the kings of the dynasties XXI and XXII. The former made it their political capital at the expense of Pi-Ramses, while the latter also elected it as their religious and funerary capital.

In those years Tanis enjoyed a time of great height, because of its strategic location as a stopover en route to Asia that made it a key point in trade with the Middle East, from whence came and departed immense wealth. It began to go into decline during the XXVI Dynasty (Saite), when economic and political axes moved toward the western delta; with new hubs such as Sais or the newly founded Greek colony of Naucratis.

Map showing the Nile Delta with some of the major ancient cities. Circled: Tanis.

However, from the 5th century AD the area of the Nile Delta began to depopulate as a result of geological and ecological changes that made life very difficult there, initiating a decline which it could not recover from. After the decline, the region became known to European researchers from the late eighteenth century, as it was briefly studied and sketched during the Napoleonic expedition of 1789. But it was not until the following century when true excavation campaigns were carried out, although at this point they were far from the modern scientific missions and were instead limited to finding a few artifacts to smuggle.

Current view of the ruins scattered throughout the tell San-el-Hagar.

An example of this activity is the attempt by the then French Consul, Bernardino Drovetti, of unearthing in 1811 two obelisks and moving them to France to give them to Napoleon, though he had to abandon the project because of its high cost. In 1825 J.J. Rifaud recovered numerous pieces in the site and made a map to indicate to Drovetti the points where he had found some of the items he took from Tanis. The English Egyptologist James Burton arrived to San el-Hagar in 1928, and from there he copied various inscriptions and drew a map;

being perhaps the first to realize the wealth of materials from the reign of Ramses II.

As in so many other places in Egypt, it would be Auguste Mariette who would take a turn to the investigations on the mound for San el-Hagar. He began to perform work there in a scientific way in 1860, followed by Flinders Petrie, who excavated between 1883 and 1886. However, the world would have to wait until 1929 for another Frenchman, Pierre Montet, to land in the ruins with the intention of performing comprehensive digging into that old stone puzzle. During numerous and intense campaigns he worked hard to unravel the secrets of a city he never even identified correctly; as he believed that Tanis, Avaris and Pi-Ramses were the same thing.

This confusion had persisted from ancient times, since Mariette himself, based on misidentification of various sculptures, had believed he found Avaris, the former capital of the Hyksos. Today we know that while they are nearby to each other, these are three clearly distinct cities.

To add to the confusion, these ruins had characteristics that made it very difficult to give a fair assessment and identification. For centuries, successive pharaohs had moved there numerous monuments, sculptures and other construction elements that were originally built in many different places in Egypt, some very distant. The most abundant materials had inscriptions in the name of Ramses II, which made it easy to confuse these ruins with those belonging to the capital of that Pharaoh, Pi-Ramses, which as we mentioned is relatively near to Tanis.

To complicate the situation even further, rainfall, more frequent in the delta than in the rest of Egypt blurred the stratigraphy; and if this were not enough, for centuries this vast field of ruins was used by local people as a quarry to supply the lime kilns, where the majority of the blocks used in the construction of monuments were used. Researchers estimate that more than 90% of the stones forming the great temple of Amun at Tanis disappeared to be consumed by these furnaces.

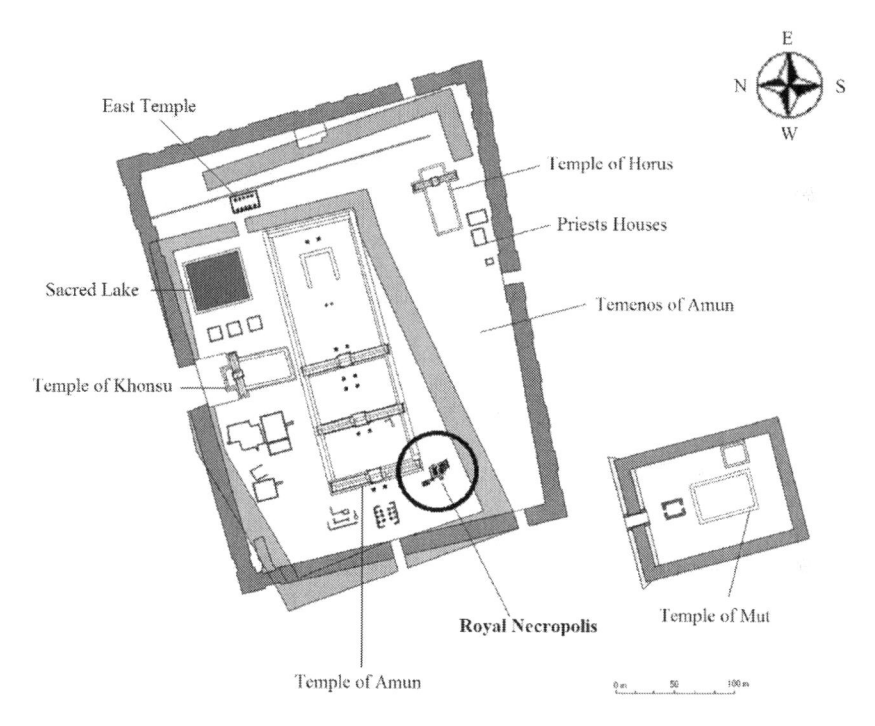

Overview of Tanis' sacred area with the main temples, most notably that of Amon, with its various construction phases. The royal necropolis appears circled. Drawing of Neithsabes, modified by the author.

Today it seems like it was an obvious attempt by the Tanite pharaohs to incorporate the reused material to build a replica of Thebes in their capital, at least with regard to religious monuments. Thus they reproduced Karnak's temple in the northern part of the Tell (temenos of

Amun and Mut), while in the south they raised the temenos of Amon of Opet in the likeness of the temple of Luxor.

One of the many statues of Ramses II found in the ruins of ancient Tanis.

An attempt to respect the Theban division is also observed: temples in the East and tombs in the West, when building the royal necropolis near the southwest corner of the Temple of Amun.

And as one would expect, in similar temples, similar gods were worshiped: the Theban triad, consisting of Amun, Mut and Khonsu was chosen as the center of Tanite worship.

Most of the archaeological missions that have worked at the site have focused their research in the area of the temples of Amun and Mut, where Montet located the royal necropolis, as this is the area that had more visible remnants from ancient times.

The temenos (sacred enclosure) of Amun and Mut is accessed by a processional avenue that once was flanked by at least 15 obelisks, coming mostly from monuments erected by Ramses II. If we consider the foundation deposits located on site, this temple was initiated by Psusennes I though, as usual, was extended by successive pharaohs.

The worship building was surrounded by a powerful wall ring, which also had to be expanded as new buildings were added. Among these extensions we find those made by Siamun and Osorkon III, who added new pylons; and Sheshonq III, who built a monumental granite entrance.

Works on San-el-Hagar did not end with Montet, because since 1965 teams of French archaeologists have continued excavating Tanis until today under the responsibility of the *Société Francaise des Fouilles de Tanis*.

View of the royal necropolis of Tanis during the excavation process. Lack of monumentality and the extensive use of recycled materials can be seen perfectly.

The Royal Necropolis and its Discovery

As we pointed out earlier, Montet was not looking for this cemetery, although he knew the possible existence of a royal necropolis in the delta thanks to the papyrus Anastasi VIII, which speaks of "the necropolis of Ramesses, beloved of Amun at the edge of the waters of Ra". Montet concluded (after the discovery of the graves) that the Tanite branch of the Nile matched these "Waters of Ra" mentioned in the papyrus. Shortly before the discovery he had found a gold amulet and fragments of funerary figurines in the name of King Osorkon in the area, which made him suspect the existence of a royal tomb nearby.

As usual, the fact that some of the tombs of this necropolis have come down to us intact is due to the combination of a series of fortunate circumstances, most notably the fact that, unlike other areas of Egypt as Thebes or Abydos, in this one we don't find a tradition of royal burials or a large noble necropolis, which would also involve less individuals dedicated to their plundering. In the case of these tombs, it also greatly helped that between the Persian and Ptolemaic times there was erected above them a number of houses, shops and chapels that would have removed the upper structures of the graves. When in turn these more modern buildings were ruined, they buried the tombs underneath them, which were then forgotten.

Current view of the royal tombs of Tanis.

Since early 1939, Montet's men were digging southwest of the temple of Amun as they wanted to study the reasons behind the deviations of a temple wall. In February, when digging in the mud floor of the buildings mentioned in the previous paragraph, several wells were found. In one of them debris was removed, and seven meters deep into this dig there appeared large stone blocks. They thought they would be the base of another building, but after continuing the removal of the tons of sand that covered them, they discovered that the huge slabs were not part of the ground construction, but the roofing of a tomb. The chosen one to verify the tomb's existence was a young man named George Goyon. He entered into the opening by being held upside-down by his feet. Unfortunately they found out that this hole they used as an access-point was the same one made by grave robbers who had plundered the tomb many centuries ago.

Yet the finding was superb, as they soon were able to see that they were not only before a royal burial, but that it also preserved important remains of grave goods.

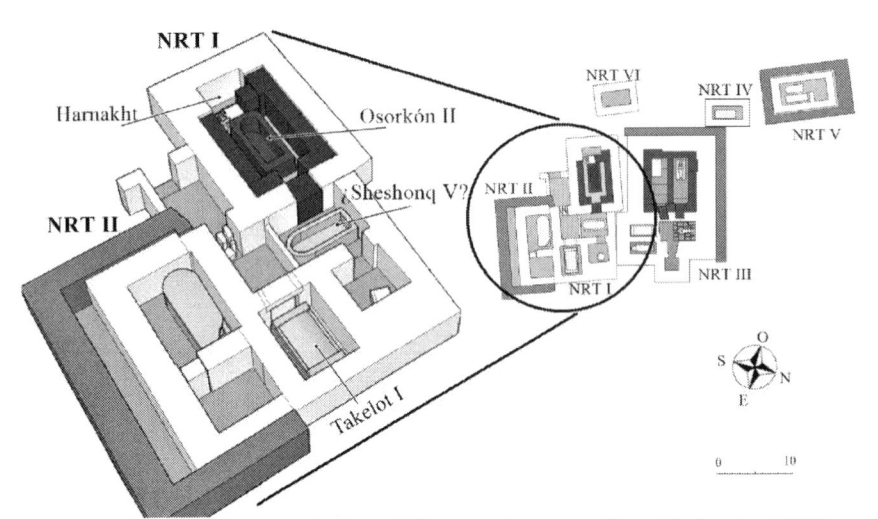

Drawing showing a general view of the royal necropolis, with tombs NRTI and NRTII expanded. Occupants of each of the chambers are indicated. Drawing of Neithsabes, modified by the author.

Osorkon II's Tomb

The first tomb studied, known as RNT I (Royal Necropolis of Tanis 1) was made up of five rooms where they had installed a total of five sarcophagi.

In the main chamber was found a huge granite sarcophagus that held the remains of the fifth pharaoh of the XXII Dynasty—Osorkon II—who reigned from about 874 to 850 BC. For the cover of the sarcophagus they had used part of a statue of Ramesside times properly trimmed. The pharaoh had been deposited in turn in a falcon-headed silver sarcophagus, of which only fragments were found. This silver sarcophagus would be similar to other recovered later in a nearby tomb containing the remains of Pharaoh Sheshonq II.

Next to the remains of Osorkon they found fragments of a wooden sarcophagus and gold jewelry and semi precious stones.

Gold figurine known as the "Triad of Osorkon," for having the name of the pharaoh engraved on the pedestal on which Osiris stands, flanked by Horus and Isis. Unknown provenance. Louvre, Paris.

The burial chamber of Osorkon is mostly covered with large granite blocks and is really small, since around the huge sarcophagus there's just a narrow corridor that leaves little room for people or grave goods; space that at the moment of the discovery was occupied by canopic vessels and more than three hundred ushebtis with the name of Osorkon.

Although Osorkon was the main occupant of the tomb, this was not the only king buried there, and it seems that other pharaohs passed through their cameras at one time or another.

And not just pharaohs, because along with Osorkon was buried Harnakht, his son, who despite having only been eight or nine at the time of his death, was first priest of Amun at Tanis. In this case the child died before the father and preceded him in the grave. To accommodate the sarcophagus of the prince (which was also reused) the tomb was enlarged by removing some granite blocks of the west wall. Inside the sarcophagus, along the remains of Harnakht were found some of the jewels he was buried with and part of the silver casket in which rested the deceased and that the thieves could not get entirely through the hole they made in the stone sarcophagus.

In another chamber of the same tomb, which had previously been redecorated, appeared the looted burial of Pharaoh Takelot I, successor of Osorkon, for which a Middle Kingdom sarcophagus was reused. One last chamber contained the remains of what may have been a secondary burial of King Sheshonq III. The possibility that Osorkon I and Sheshonq V could have passed through this tomb is not ruled out, as there appeared some objects and evidence of their presence. If it is confirmed then this would be what Egyptologists would call a *cachette;* a burial in which several bodies from other graves are gathered—moved there for different reasons.

This tomb put on the table several issues that puzzled researchers for a long time. One such issue was the paradox that while it appeared that the tomb of Osorkon had been built before that of Psusennes (NRT-III), since the latter had to adapt to the space left by the previous one; the occupants of NRT-III belonged to the XXI dynasty, i.e., they reigned before the pharaohs resting at NRT-I, which belonged to the subsequent XXII dynasty. This led to some archaeologists to defend a change in the royal lists to accommodate the new chronological order that these tombs seemed to indicate.

Eventually, however, everything seemed to suggest that the solution to this puzzle was much simpler: they had simply discovered a reoccupation of old graves by new tenants, something that matches marvelously with the spirit of Tanis, the Egyptian capital of recycling and reuse. Let's not forget that all the stones used for the construction of the tombs are from earlier monuments, mostly from Ramesside times. Moreover, it seems that this tomb was originally built for Pharaoh Smendes (1069-1043 BC), but Osorkon II occupied it after adapting it to his needs by adding new decor, introducing a new sarcophagus for himself and knocking down part of the west wall of his own chamber to make room inside for his son. It also amended the lobby of the tomb, where he settled another sarcophagus for his father.

But despite being a discovery of such a magnitude, the best was yet to come, and it was on March 17th, 1939 that they had to stop work on the tomb of Osorkon II, as an even more spectacular discovery had taken place a few meters from the previous one.

Archaeologists had lifted a thick slab of rock that revealed another burial chamber. When penetrating through the hole they reached a kind of well, and behind a wall a small corridor opened, and on the other side they could see what no archaeologist had seen before: the first fully intact royal tomb of Egypt, since we must remember that even the famous tomb of Tutankhamun, despite the fantastic treasures it contained, had suffered at least two intrusions.

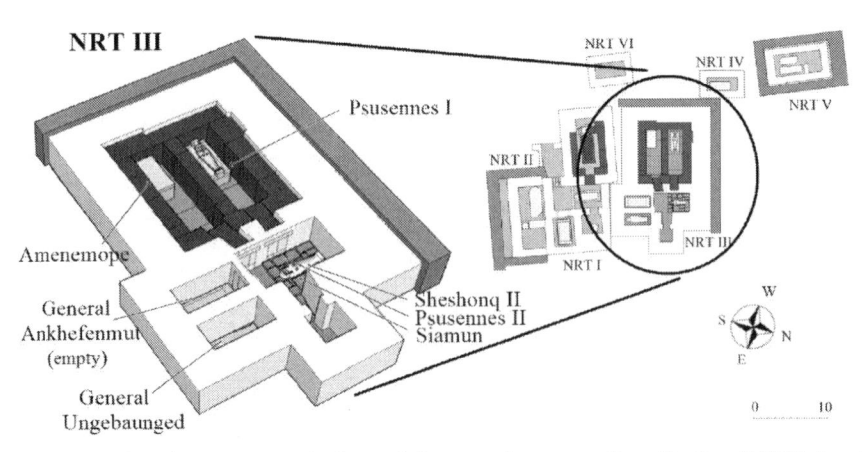

Drawing showing a general view of the royal necropolis with the NRTIII tomb extended. Occupants of each of the chambers are indicated. Drawing of Neithsabes, modified by the author.

The Tomb of Psusennes I

"Our eyes were accustomed gradually, now we could see the dark depths of a room. [...] What we saw then filled us with admiration ... The dream! The legendary dream of every archaeologist [...] to see open before him the true cave of Ali Baba. The dream had come true! [...] Before us, on the floor, we vaguely distinguished lots of mixed objects of which emerged the glittering of gold. A series of stone and alabaster vessels, including canopic jars still standing against the wall. On the right, a black shape with purple reflections laid on a stone platform. A statue? It looked more like a mummy container, yes, a sort of anthropomorphic sarcophagus, but topped with the head of a bird, a so unusual tomb that nothing like it was known in the archaeological records. A crack in the side of the casket let out reflections from polished, shiny gold, unaltered, as new [...] ". (Goyon (G.) The discovery of the treasures of Tanis, Paris, 2004).

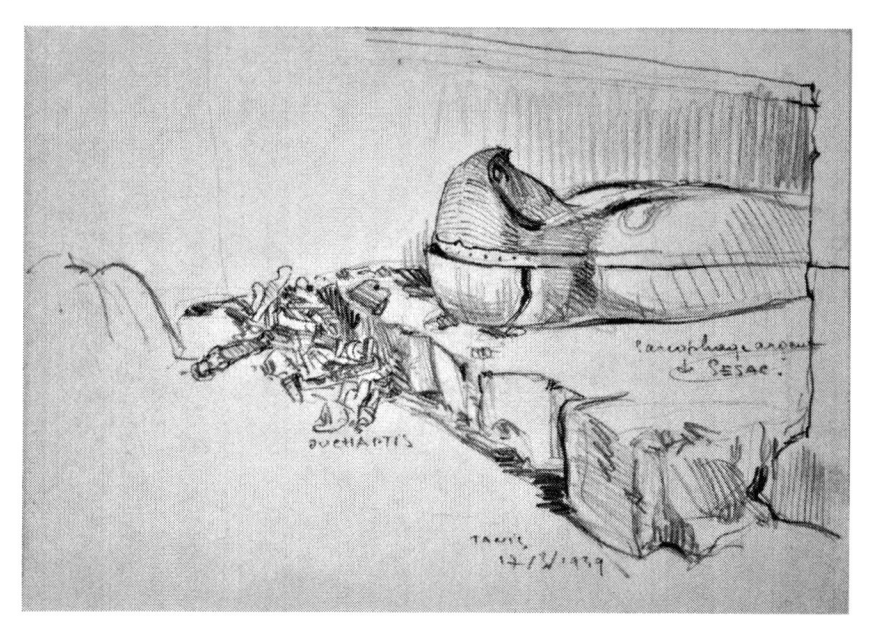

Sketch showing the location of the silver coffin of Pharaoh Sheshonq II and ushebtis that were piled beside it, just as their discoverers found them. The date 17-03-1939 can be seen perfectly. Drawing of Pierre Montet.

As Montet's assistant George Goyon tells us, the first thing they saw was a strange sarcophagus with a falcon head covered with dust and debris, resting on stone blocks. They soon discovered that it was made entirely of silver. On both sides of the sarcophagus there were two skeletons, but only some gold leaves of the external decoration remained from the wooden sarcophagus that had contained them, and those leaves adorned now, in a macabre way, the bones of the two men, who also retained some jewelry. Researchers believe that these two bodies are those of pharaohs Siamun and Psusennes II.

Alongside the skeletons were multiple pieces of funerary equipment, including canopic vessels and a small mountain formed by hundreds of "ushebtis"; figurines of servants that would have to do the work of the deceased in the afterlife.

On the walls of the burial chamber one could read a name: Psusennes I, but something didn't quite add up.

> "That's when the inscription carved on the central band of the sarcophagus appeared, with cartridges containing the royal protocol I had the pleasure of deciphering first" Héqakheperrê Chéchanq beloved of Amun," I read aloud. Montet got angry: "You must have misread, we know of no king of this name," he said." (Goyon (G.) the discovery of the treasures of Tanis, Paris, 2004)

The name on the sarcophagus belonged to an unknown pharaoh different to the tomb's owner.

Given the magnitude of the discovery it was immediately decided to close the tomb until a proper security system could be established, for which the next day several soldiers and an officer were sent from Cairo to install it.

The discovery was of such a level that king Farouk himself decided to attend the March 21st opening of the silver sarcophagus and the organizing of the tomb's inventory.

> "The next day, in the presence of King Farouk [...] Together we lifted the lid of the silver sarcophagus. That's when it appeared in all its beauty, set by the magic of incorruptible metal, the gold mask, the radiant image of Pharaoh Héqakheperré-Chéchanq [...] This beautiful mask, whipped into a plate of pure gold of a millimeter thick, was not only a wonderful piece of jewelry, but also a historical document of the first order [...] "(Goyon (G.) the discovery of the treasures of Tanis, Paris, 2004)

The royal mummy was inside a golden *cartonnage* with face covered by a mask in the shape of falcon's head made of gold foil. All the organic parts were in very bad condition, so they had to be consolidated, work done by Alfred Lucas, the same man who worked on the tomb of Tutankhamun. What it had kept in perfect condition were the large number of jewelries such as the king's necklaces, pectorals, earrings, bracelets and rings. As was customary, the fingers and toes were covered with gold caps and wore sandals, also of gold.

One of the pectorals of gold, lapis lazuli and faience found in the tomb of Sheshonq II. Egyptian Museum in Cairo.

Once consolidated, the contents of the chamber were transferred to the Cairo Museum, so the next step could start: the opening of the burial chambers that where on the back of the lobby and that were closed by two granite blocks.

The northernmost section, with its access blocked by a section of an obelisk of Rameses II, proved to be the one containing the body of Psusennes I, the original owner of the tomb, resting in a pink granite sarcophagus located at the bottom of the compartment surrounded by a huge number of artifacts he was buried with. Unfortunately the weather, which was much more humid than that of the Valley of the Kings, had done away with most of objects made of perishable materials, depriving us of valuable information.

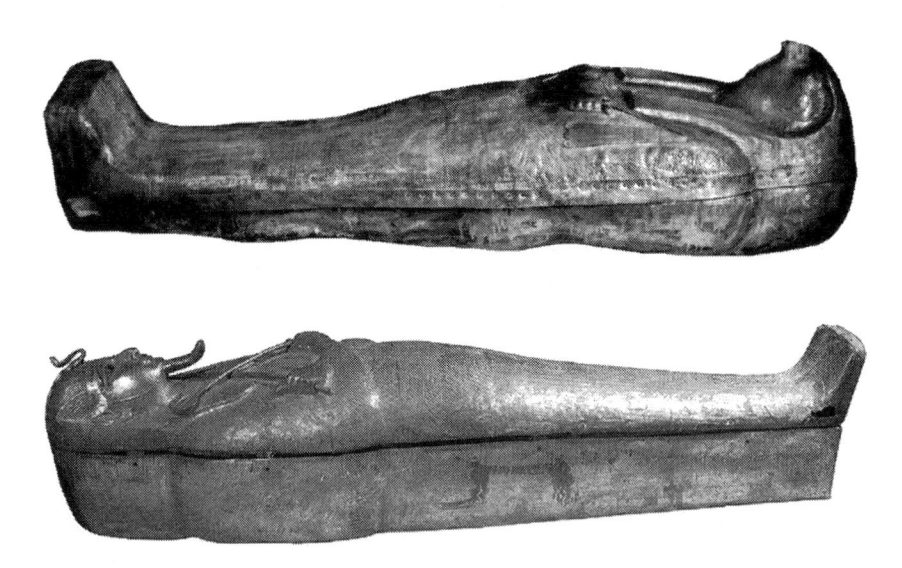

The two magnificent silver coffins located in the NRTIII tomb: the one above, falcon-headed, contained the mummy of Sheshonq II, while the bottom one kept the remains of Psusennes I. Egyptian Museum in Cairo.

The sarcophagus was reused and had belonged to Merenptah, pharaoh of the nineteenth dynasty and successor of the great Ramses II, and on it there was still preserved a scepter made of gold and wood deposited at the time of burial.

Inside, there was a second anthropoid sarcophagus of black granite also reused, although we don't know its original owner. This second sarcophagus still kept another also anthropomorphic one, but this completely made of silver, showing the king's face covered with the *Nemes* and a solid gold *uraeus* on its forehead.

Extraordinary gold mask that covered the head and chest of Pharaoh Psusennes I. Reminds of Tutankhamun's. Egyptian Museum in Cairo.

When opening it they found a gold mask covering the king's head extending to the chest. This mask was reminiscent of that of Tutankhamun, although the boy Pharaoh's had lots of inlaid carnelian, glass paste, turquoise, etc., which gave it a very colorful appearance, while that of Psusennes only used lapis lazuli for highlighting the beard, eyebrows and eyes, while the rest shows only the color of gold, which has a dull sheen, as it wasn't polished.

The pharaoh's mummy was covered up to a foot by a gold foil embossed with decorative motifs similar to those of the silver sarcophagus. And another silver foil separated the body of the king from the bottom of the sarcophagus.

The jewels adorning the mummy are magnificent, and among them are six gold necklaces, one of which has a cuneiform inscription; it was the gift of a grand vizier of Syria to one of his daughters, which was probably sent to Psusennes' harem.

Necklace and pectorales found on the mummy of Psusennes I. They are just a sampling of the dozens of jewels of gold and semi precious stones that adorned the body of the dead pharaoh. Egyptian Museum in Cairo.

The ornamentation was completed with pectorals of gold and precious stones, twenty bracelets adorning her arms and legs, rings and earrings, as well as the traditional gold plate covering the cut made on the left side through which the Pharaoh's guts had been removed during mummification.

Before the sarcophagus were deposited cups, bowls and plates of gold and silver, many ushebtis, scepters and weapons, of which only some metal parts remained: including arrowheads, shield umbones, sword handles, etc.

It is a truly exceptional collection that we enjoy today in the Cairo Museum.

Golden mask that covered the head and part of the chest of Pharaoh Amenemope. It can be seen how the artistic quality is far from those of the masks of Tutankhamun and Psusennes. Egyptian Museum in Cairo.

Amenemope's Tomb

As soon as works were completed in Psusennes' chamber, archaeologists set out to open the chamber next to it, so they had to expand that year's campaign. They didn't want to leave an intact tomb waiting for months. It was just too tempting for thieves, a risk they couldn't take.

The decoration on the wall that blocked the door showed Psusennes' mother: Queen Mutnegemet, but her name had been replaced by that of King Amenemope, Psusennes's successor. The granite sarcophagus had also suffered the same change in the name of its occupant and in this case it had only contained a single gilded wooden sarcophagus, of which there were only a few remnants around the king's body.

On the head and hands of the mummy there had been placed a thick gold foil and a mask, also of gold, covering the head and chest. A significant number of jewelry were visible on the pharaoh's body, although less than in the case of Psusennes. Alongside the sarcophagus was the rest of the outfit that consisted of: the ushebtis, tableware of silver and bronze and four alabaster canopic jars without lids.

We don't know the reason for the presence of this pharaoh in the tomb of Psusennes' mother, since Amenemope had his own grave in the same cemetery; a simple limestone chamber plundered since ancient times in which only a few funerary figurines were found alongside the sarcophagus itself, with the pink granite top reused from another much older one, perhaps even of the Fourth Dynasty. It is possible that the body of the pharaoh was moved to its final location in an attempt to prevent its desecration, although it was only moved by around a dozen meters, so that the security conditions vary very little. This is one of the mysteries that still surrounds this finding.

Remember that while these archaeological works were underway, more and more countries were involved in WWII and they grew daily in virulence, so that after the transfer of all the pieces to

Cairo, the excavation was closed, and would not be resumed until 1945.

Though a guard was in charge of monitoring the tombs, thieves acted again, stirring Psusennes' tomb and looking for some leftover valuables to pillage. Most damaging was the 1943 theft of Psusennes' jewels, which were kept in a safe in the basement of the Cairo Museum. Although almost all the stolen pieces were recovered, some pieces were lost forever.

Gold mask of general Wendjebwaendjed, whose burial chamber was the last to be located in the tomb of Psusennes. Its rich trousseau was worthy of a king. Egyptian Museum.

The Last Secrets of Psusennes' Tomb

On April 15, 1945, when the war was in its last throes, Montet went back to Tanis, though only accompanied by his daughter and George Goyon. His idea was to continue exploring Psusennes' tomb, as he was sure he hadn't yet discovered all its secrets. In the southern wall of the antechamber he found an opening to another burial chamber that was ready to receive general Ankhefenmut in a granite sarcophagus also reused. On the walls of the tomb appeared his name followed by his many titles, "Grand Steward of Amun, Great Commander of the Horses of Amun, First Great Squire of His Majesty, Prophet of Mut, Lady of Isheru." The accumulation of so many honors, the fact that he shared the royal burial, and some inscriptions that were found, would suggest that he was a prince, a son of Psusennes himself. But the sarcophagus appeared empty, and there was not a single piece of the grave goods inside the chamber.

In the following year, yet another tomb was discovered (next to the previous one), when Montet no longer directed the excavation. Alexandre Lezine found the burial chamber of the General Wendjebwaendjed decorated with brightly painted reliefs that quickly faded as soon as the tomb was opened and the atmosphere, which had remained unchanged for nearly 3000 years, was modified.

Wendjebwaendjed also rested in a second-hand sarcophagus, which in this case had belonged to a priest of Amun at Thebes, though it seemed that its new owner didn't like the original decoration, since they covered it with stucco and made a new one, to which they then added a golden finish.

Within the granite sarcophagus appeared some remains of another one of timber in which Wendjebwaendjed had been buried, in turn inside a silver sarcophagus of which they were only able to recover some badly damaged fragments. What was kept in perfect condition was the golden mask covering the General's face, the gold covers of fingers and toes, and amulets and jewels adorning its body, which included three breastplates, two bracelets and several rings, all made of gold. The funerary equipment was completed with crockery of gold and silver, various weapons and, of course, its canopic jars, made of alabaster and with lids in the form of human heads.

Unfortunately we have no photographs showing the work inside the tombs or of the artifacts and parts in their original positions in the style of the extraordinary images that Harry Burton took in Tutankhamun's tomb. Perhaps the background of the war prompted the team to hastily remove all material from the burial chambers faster than advisable. Likewise the meticulous work of scale drawing all the material before moving it, which was done in Tut's tomb, was put aside in this case.

Therefore we have to settle almost exclusively with the written descriptions of Montet and Goyon.

One of the plates found in the tomb of General Wendjebwaendjed. It is made of silver with some gold additions and has a simple and delicate decoration. Egyptian Museum in Cairo.

Old photograph of the hypostyle hall of the temple of Amun at Karnak. The powerful Theban clergy became a formidable rival for the weak Pharaohs of the XX Dynasty reaching to snatch the kings part of their powers.

Who were these Pharaohs?

The Third Intermediate Period and the Dynasties XXI and XXII

As mentioned above, the pharaohs buried in Tanis belonged to the dynasties XXI and XXII, which in turn are framed in the so-called Third Intermediate Period, a time of instability and fragmentation of power.

Throughout the twentieth dynasty, the power of the pharaohs had been weakened in an important way. On the one hand the pharaohs gave more and more territory to the temples, especially that of Amun in Thebes, and a time came when the first priests of this temple rivaled in power with the kings. On the other hand, there emerged new, excessively powerful political groups that undermined the royal authority. One of these groups was the Libyans, who had originally come as prisoners of war and were settled in previous centuries in military colonies; but over time they became fully fledged Egyptians, without losing their identities, and their influence grew continuously until they started bringing some of their people to the throne.

The situation erupted during the reign of Ramses II, last king of the XX Dynasty, when power was divided into two fractions: The first was Upper Egypt under the command of the first priest of Amun at Thebes, who controlled the valley of the Nile. Its first ruler was Herior, who used royal titles, and who would be succeeded by his son Piankh. From this, the Theban priests would recognize the Tanite pharaohs and even some would eventually marry women from the royal family, but would govern the south completely independently.

Meanwhile in Lower Egypt, at the death of Ramses XI, Smendes rose to the throne and started the XXI Dynasty, known as Tanite after transferring their capital to Tanis, in the Delta, and in which the Libyan component was very important. The other pharaohs of this dynasty would be Amenemnisu, Psusennes I, Amenemope, Osokhor, Siamon and Psusennes II.

Sheshonq I, who was married to a daughter of Psusennes II, started the XXII Dynasty with kings of Libyan origin. His successor was Osorkon I, accompanied at the end of his reign as regent for Seshonq II, who died without ever governing alone. Other pharaohs of this dynasty were Takelot I, Osorkon II, Takelot II and his son Osorkon III, First Priest of Amun at Thebes, who also assumed the kingship by force of arms and with which the XXII dynasty would end after continuous power struggles and a deep internal division.

Gold plat that was sewn between the bandages of the mummy of Pharaoh Psusennes I, just above the incision through which the viscera were removed during the mummification process. Its function was the magical protection of the deceased. Egyptian Museum in Cairo.

Tanis Burials

Psusennes I.- Was the third Pharaoh of the XXI Dynasty, and seems to have had a long and successful reign, although the exact duration is far from clear (c. 1036/989 BC). He had a brief co-regency with his predecessor Amenemnisu, and improved relations with the priests of Thebes marrying one of his daughters with the first priest of Amun in that city. He emerged as the chief priest of Amun at Tanis.

Amenemope.- He was the son of Psusennes I, with whom he shared power for a couple of years as co-regent. The length of his reign is unclear, although Manetho ascribes him only nine years, from 993 to 984 BC, a priest mummy in Thebes dates from the year 49 of the reign of the pharaoh. Few monuments of Amenemope are known, one of them is his own grave in the royal necropolis of Tanis from which, as stated above, was moved at an undetermined time, perhaps during the reign of Siamun, and taken to the grave of his father, where he was deposited in his mother's sarcophagus, Queen Mutnegemet. Studies on his mummy have concluded that he was lame and could have died of meningitis at around the age of 50.

Siamun.- One of the most powerful kings of the XXI Dynasty, apparently reigned 19 years, between 986 and 967 BC. We know little of his family, but it has left signs of a major construction activity in the temples, especially in that of Ammon in Tanis, but also in Memphis.

During his reign the first priest of Amun at Thebes, Pinedjem II organized the transfer of the royal mummies located in Deir el Bahari's *Cachette* to save them from looting that had spread through the Valley of the Kings.

Psusennes II.- Last pharaoh of the XXI Dynasty, reigned between approximately 959 and 945 BC. Also little is known of him, and we have learned about only a few monuments of his reign.

It seems he had been first priest of Amun at Thebes, afterwards reaching the royal dignity upon the death of Pharaoh Siamun, becoming King of Upper and Lower Egypt, reunified again, at least nominally, since the effective control of the different regions was held more by powerful local families.

Sheshonq II.- There are many questions surrounding this pharaoh, who was unknown until his body was found in the antechamber of the tomb of Psusennes I. It seems he was the son of Osorkon I, which would have associated him with the throne around the year 890 BC, although it seems that the child died before the father, for which he would not have come to reign alone.

Osorkon II.- He reigned from 874 to 850 BC He placed his kids in key religious positions, one of them, Harnakht, was the first priest of Amun at Tanis; when he died while still a child was buried in the same chamber that Osorkon had prepared for himself.

Views of an alabaster urn with cartouche of pharaoh Osorkon II, found in the Phoenician necropolis of Cerro San Cristobal-Laurita (Almuñécar, Granada-Spain), where it was used as a funerary urn. Archaeological Museum of Granada.

This king undertook a major construction activity, primarily in Bubastis, but also at Thebes, Memphis and Tanis, where he used mainly building materials reused from Pi-Ramesses.

Takelot II.- He reigned from 860 to 835 BC, during a period of great instability, among other things because he named his son Osorkon as the first priest of Amun at Thebes, which was not accepted there, thus erupting a civil war.

Sarcophagus located in the same chamber that housed the remains of Osorkon II, and containing the remains of his son Harnakht. Tanis.

Wendjebwaendjed.- Very important character in the court of Psusennes I that lived around 1000 BC. He had many different titles, both military and civilian, including "the King's treasurer, solely responsible for the praises of the great organized ceremonies to reward courage, the Keeper of the Seal of the King of Lower Egypt, Chief of the Navy, First Bowman of the Pharaoh, Mayor of Khonsu in Thebes, etc."

Detail of the black granite sarcophagus reused by Pharaoh Psusennes I. We don't know who was his original owner. Egyptian Museum in Cairo.

Conclusion

It is often said that the key of success is to be in the right place at the right time; this is evident in the history of the discovery of the royal tombs of Tanis, one of the biggest success stories of archaeology of all time, but is unknown by most of the public because it came at the worst possible moment, just when the world faced in astonishment the beginning of one of the largest military confrontations known so far to humanity.

Too often it's emphasized that this finding included the only three royal tombs found intact so far, as a reminder that Tutankhamun's tomb was not intact, but had suffered at least two intrusions in ancient times. But we must be aware that despite the thefts, the riches of the tomb of the Child King far outweigh the treasures of the Tanite necropolis. This is so for two main reasons: first, due to the fact that the exceptional preservation of objects from Tut's tomb allowed us to enjoy elements made of perishable materials, some of them as fragile as ostrich feather fans that were found in some boxes. This didn't happen in the tombs of Tanis, where the humid environment of the delta destroyed coffins, mummies and many objects made of nonmetallic materials. The other reason is political, because the weakness of the kings of the Third Intermediate Period didn't allow the accumulation of wealth that we see in the past. Even their graves are more than modest, and manufactured based on elements reused from other buildings.

Despite the silver coffins and gold masks these tombs are a true reflection of a moment of decline of kings unable to re-unify the country under a single ruler as their predecessors had done, and not only that, but with them; the end of Egyptian culture would begin, because from that moment all the pharaohs would be foreign. No Egyptian would again occupy the throne of the unified Upper and Lower Egypt. Libyans, Nubians, Persians, Greeks and Romans would eventually rise to power in the country of the Nile, on a downward path that would lead inexorably to the demise of this ancient culture.

Dear reader, I want to spend my last few lines to thank you for choosing my book and for reaching the end of its reading, which hopefully means that you liked it. If so, I would ask you to dedicate one minute to review it at Amazon to help other readers find what they seek.
Best regards, I hope we meet again in my next work.

http:// benjamincollado.com

Lost (and Found) Pharaohs

Bibliography:

First Book

- BAINES, J. y MALEK, J. Dioses, templos y faraones. Madrid, 1992.
- BELOVA, G. "TT320 and the History of the Royal Cache During the Twenty-first Dynasty", pp. 73-80, Egyptology at the Dawn of the Twenty-first Century 1, El Cairo, 2003.
- CABANAS, A. Los secretos de Osiris, Madrid, 2006.
- CARTER, H. "Report on the Robbery of the Tomb of Amenotes II, Biban el-Molouk". ASAE, nº 3, pp. 61001-61044. El Cairo, 1902.
- CARTER, H. La tumba de Tutankhamon, Barcelona, 1985.
- CERAM, C.W. Dioses, tumbas y sabios, Barcelona, 1985.
- DARESSY, G. "Les sepultures des prètres d'Ammon à Deir el Bahari", ASAE, núm. 1, pp. 141-148. El Cairo, 1900.
- DESROCHES-NOBLECOURT, C. Ramsés II: la verdadera historia. Destino, Barcelona, 2004.
- DODSON, A. y HILTON, D. *The Complete Royale Families of Ancient Egypt*, Thames & Hudson, 2004.
- GRAEFE, E. *"La cachette royale de Deir el-Bahari 1998-2003-2004-2005* pp.7-12, Égypte, Afrique et Orient 38, 2005.
- GRAEFE, E. "The Royal Cache and the Tomb Robberies", pp. 74-82, en The Theban Necropolis, Past Present and Future, N. Strudwick and J.H. Taylor, Londres, 2003.
- LORET. V. "Le tombeau d'Amenophis et la chachette royale de Biban el-Molouk". BIE, nº 3, pp.91-97. El Cairo, 1899
- MASPERO, G. La Trouvalle de Deir el Bahari. El Cairo, 1881.
- MASPERO, G. LEROUX, E. Les Momies royales de Deir el Bahari. París, 1889.
- PARRA, J.M. El imperio egipcio. RBA-National Geographic Society. Barcelona, 2013.
- REEVES, N. y WILKINSON, R.H. *Das Tal der Könige*, Bechtermünz Augsburg, 2002.
- SHAW, I. (ed.) Historia del Antiguo Egipto. La Esfera de los Libros. Madrid, 2010.

- VERCOUTTER, J. Egipto, tras las huellas de los faraones. Aguilar Universal. Madrid, 1989.
- VV.AA. Los grandes descubrimientos de la Arqueología, Volúmenes I y II. Barcelona, 1988.

Second Book

– BAINES, J. y MALEK, J. Dioses, templos y faraones. Madrid, 1992.
– CARNARVON et al. Five years' explorations at Thebes: a record of work done 1907–1911. London, 1912
– CARTER, H. La tumba de Tutankhamon, Barcelona, 1985.
– CERAM, C.W. Dioses, tumbas y sabios, Barcelona, 1985.
– DODSON, A. y HILTON, D. The Complete Royale Families of Ancient Egypt, Thames & Hudson, 2004.
– HAWASS, Z. ed. Egyptology at the Dawn of the Twenty-first Century: El Cairo, 2003.
– HOVING, T. Tutankhamun: The Untold Story. 1978
– IKRAM S. "Some Thoughts on the Mummification of King Tutankhamun". Études et Travaux, XXVI, 291-301. 2013
– JAMES, T. G. H. Howard Carter: The Path to Tutankhamun, 2001.
– JAMES, T. G. H. Tutankamon, Barcelona, 2005.
– MARCHANT J. The Shadow King: The Bizarre Afterlife of King Tut's Mummy. 2013
– REVERTE COMAS, J.M. La maldición de los faraones, Madrid, 1993.
– VERCOUTTER, J. Egipto, tras las huellas de los faraones, Madrid, 1898.
– VV.AA. Los grandes descubrimientos de la Arqueología, Volúmenes I y II. Barcelona, 1988.

Third Book

– DODSON, A. y HILTON, D. The Complete Royale Families of Ancient Egypt, Thames & Hudson, 2004.
– GOYON, G. La découverte des trésors de Tanis. París, 2004.
– HAWASS, Z. ed. Egyptology at the Dawn of the Twenty-first Century: El Cairo, 2003.
– KITCHEN, K.A. The Third Intermediate Period (1100-650 B.B.), Warminster, 1973.
– MONTET, P. et allii. "Les constructions et le tombeau de Pseusennes à

Tanis", Syria, París, 1951.

– MONTET, P. et allii. "Les constructions et le tombeau d'Osorkon II à Tanis", Syria, París, 1947.

– VERCOUTTER, J. Egipto, tras las huellas de los faraones, Madrid, 1898.

– VV.AA. Los grandes descubrimientos de la Arqueología, Volúmenes I y II. Barcelona, 1988.

– ZIEGLER, C. Les tresors de Tanis, capitale oubliee des pharaons de l'an mille. París, 2001.

Webpages:

www.thebanmappingproject.com
Depends on the American University in Cairo and has plans and complete and reliable information about the graves and monuments in the area of Thebes.

http://anubis4_2000.tripod.com/mummypages1/introduction.htm
Excellent site of William Max Miller that studies one by one the most famous Egyptian mummies, with lots of data, images and bibliography.

http://www.narmer.pl
Very complete page of Dariusz Sitek that includes information on chronologies, tombs, pharaohs, maps, bibliography etc.

Photograps by

Félix Bonfils: pág. 4 y 206; Hnos Zangaky: 10; M. Delie y E. Bechard: 22; Nadar: 25; Captmondo: 30; Biblioteca-Museo Víctor Balaguer: 31; Ernesto Graf: 37; Howard Frost: 44; Emil Brugsch: 46, 47, 57 y 60; Benjamín Collado: 50 y 73; María Young: 63; Miroslav Tarkouski: 64;

Dto. Antigüedades Egipcias de El Cairo: 65 y 67; Quaderns Digitals: 70; Daderot: 74; Michael R. Hogarth: 80; Howard Carter: 88; Samuel Foster: 95; Harry Burton: 102, 106, 113, 116, 118, 123, 129, 131, 133, 134, 136 y 137; Dominique Plateau: 110; Ismail Salem: 127; Richard Hull: 141; Fáctum Arte: 144; Valerie Bouchard: 152; James Klim: 160; Kelly James: 164; Abdul Mutaal: 168; Victoria Chan: 170; C. Ziegler: 172; Pierre Montet: 177, 184, 196, 198, 202, 205 y 201; George Moulin: 179; Einsamer Schütze: 182 y 212; Gus Gleiter: 186; Guillaume Blanchard: 189; John Campana: 199; Paul Stewart: 195; John Haig: 197; Christian Lenz: 209; I. De la Torre: 211; Einsamer Schütze: 212 y Simon Hayter: 214.

The author has made every effort to get permission from the owners of the rights of the non-free images, having been achieved in most cases. Yet there are some in which it has been impossible to identify the author or copyright owner. Please, if you are the author of any of these images I beg you to contact the author. Thank you.

Benjamin Collado Hinarejos

Lost (and Found) Pharaohs

Printed in Great Britain
by Amazon